RACHEL ASHWELL'S
SHABBY CHIC

A Fleamarket Stall

An Antique Mall

A Yard Sale

TREASURE HUNTING
& DECORATING GUIDE

PHOTOGRAPHY BY WYNN MILLER & CATHY MOGULL
ILLUSTRATIONS BY DEBORAH GREENFIELD

GRAPHIC DESIGN BY GABRIELLE RAUMBERGER & CLIFFORD SINGONTIKO

ReganBooks
An Imprint of HarperCollins*Publishers*

150% enlargement

for dresser in bedroom.

Argile Rose   Lavande Grisée   Vert

Rose Burgundy 1   Lavande   Vert

Rose Burgundy 2   Sky Blue   Pine

Wine   Sea Blue   Peacock

RACHEL ASHWELL'S SHABBY CHIC. Copyright © 1998 by Rachel Ashwell.
All rights reserved. Printed in Hong Kong. No part of this book may be used or reproduced
in any manner whatsoever without written permission except in the case of
brief quotations embodied in critical articles and reviews. For information address
HarperCollins Publishers, Inc., 10 East 53rd Street, New York, NY 10022.

HarperCollins books may be purchased for educational, business, or sales promotional use.
For information please write: Special Markets Department,
HarperCollins Publishers, Inc., 10 East 53rd Street, New York, NY 10022

FIRST EDITION

Designed by Gabrielle Raumberger Design, Santa Monica, California:
Gabrielle Raumberger and Clifford Singontiko

Additional photo credits: Rosalind Simon, pp. 5, 46 and 47, 44 and 45

The floral arrangements that appear in the photographs of Bountiful are
courtesy of Bryan Wark.

ISBN 0-06-039208-8

Cataloging-in-Publication Data on file at the Library of Congress

02 ❖ 10 9

To Mum and Dad

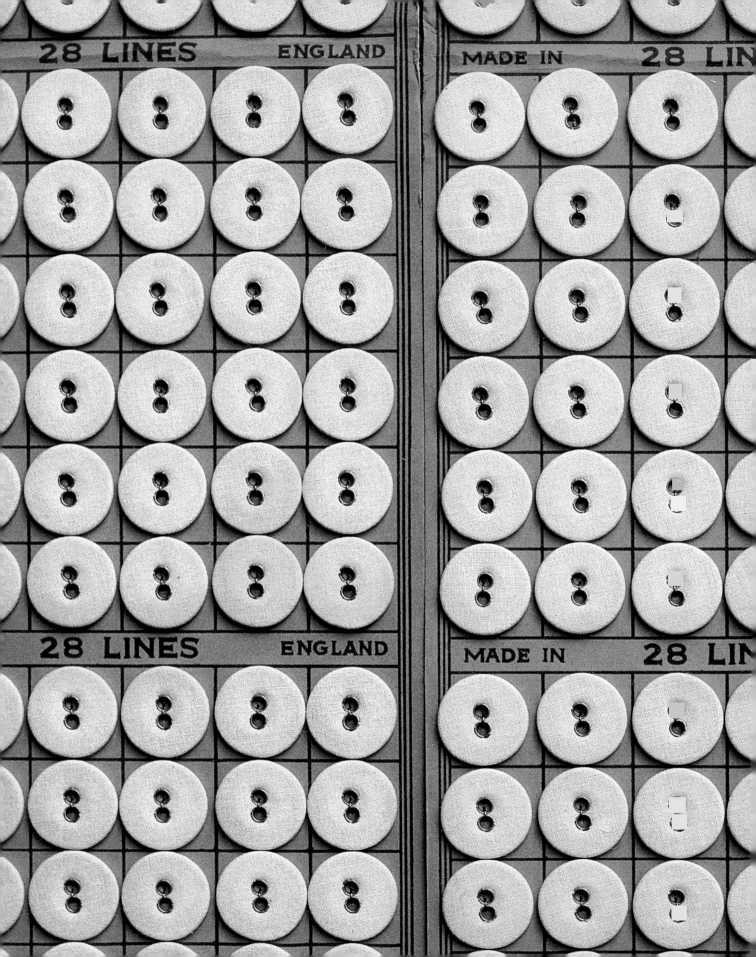

CONTENTS

ACKNOWLEDGMENTS

Shabby Chic is about comfort and awareness of what is truly important and valuable. This description is also true of the following people to whom I owe thanks and appreciation for their various contributions to this book.

Thank you, Cathy, for your lovely photographs and for bringing me Wynn.

Wynn, for your patience, support, and your photographs, too.

Gabrielle and Cliff, for understanding my vision.

Deborah, my sister, for your wonderful, charming illustrations.

Annabel Davis-Goff, for giving grace to my mumbled text.

Brendan and Rochelle, for your truly endless perseverance with the captions.

Mari, Rodney, Tom , Elliot, Julie, Sonny, Marilyn, Georgann, Nina, Jeanne, Jenni, Helena, Linda, Mark, Damon, Kevin, Kinga, Jeff, Miguel, Julian, Manuel, Helen, Petty, Terry, Camilla, Rosetta, Kristin, Kerry, Stephanie, Claudine, and Lupe.
Your support of Shabby Chic allows me to do what I love to do.

Linda, for understanding my love of the shade of pink.

Tinda, for your attention to detail.

Angelica, Jenny, and Judith, thank you for loving what I love.

Andrea and Bruce, M.L., Sue, Barry and Lili, Nina and Lou, Liz, and Karin, for welcoming me in to your homes and sharing your worlds.

Ted, for your unique point of view that inspires me.

And lastly, thank you to Lili and Jake, for understanding the days of my preoccupation with the "book."

RACHEL ASHWELL'S
SHABBY CHIC

TREASURE HUNTING
& DECORATING GUIDE

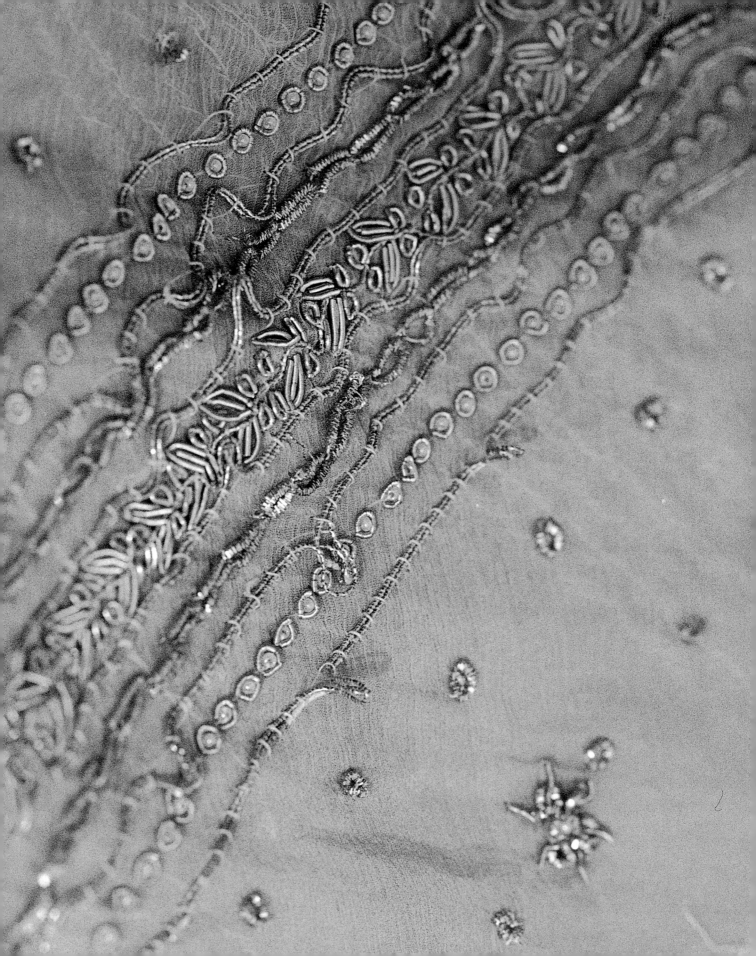

INTRODUCTION

introduction

Early mornings at flea markets: a childhood memory. I still feel that flutter of excitement—not entirely acquisitive—that I used to feel as a small girl, arriving at the flea market with my parents on cold mornings. We would rise in the dark, dress sleepily, and hurried by my mother, we would arrive at the market as the vendors were unpacking their wares. I remember those vendors as though they were distant relatives. And I remember the smell of the cakes from the cafeteria, and the accelerated speed at which my father walked when he had the whiff of a treasure.

Now I live, with my own children, in Malibu, in a house where, when I wake, the sound of the ocean replaces the hum of traffic on the London street where I was born. And visits to a flea market are not only a voyage into the past of the object I inspect and sometimes buy and restore but a journey into my own childhood.

My mother bought, restored, and sold antique dolls and teddy bears. My father dealt in secondhand rare books. My parents took my sister and me with them on those flea-market Sunday mornings, and without planning it, they opened the door to a glimpse of cultural history. In doing so, they also gave me a head start in developing my "eye" and, later, the means of earning my living.

3

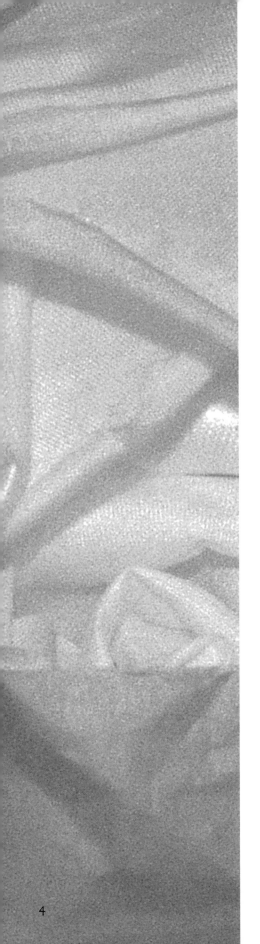

My mother would advertise in local newspapers around the country: "Dolls and teddy bears wanted." Before she set off to a prospective seller she would talk to him for a long time on the telephone, mostly to discuss the type of doll or bear offered for sale but also to be sure the owner was really ready to part with a childhood friend. My mother was not an aggressive buyer. She was honest about her intentions and would lovingly restore the dolls and bears, knowing that ultimately they would be sold—to (she hoped) good homes.

I can remember waiting in excited anticipation for her to come home from her buying trips. She usually traveled by train, with her finds packed in a suitcase or bags. After she had revived herself with a cup of tea, she would carefully unwrap the layers of tissue paper protecting the porcelain heads of the dolls. On a certain level, this was quite an

Dolls' bloomers
19th

intimate business. Often, as she unwrapped her purchases, sometimes she would tell me their history. After the dolls, she would unwrap their accessories. I was fascinated by the tiny clothes and scrunched-up silk flowers, hanging by threads from the straw hats and the matted wigs.

At this point, my mother would assess what could be saved, restored, or left as is. By watching this process of assessment, I developed the ability to judge items that cross my path.

I rarely wanted to own any of the treasures my mother brought home. But I was intrigued and developed an appreciation of quality, detail, patience, function, and beauty.

The imperfect dolls, often the less-fussy boy dolls, were my personal favorites. A doll with a cracked face or some fingers missing was the seed of the "imperfect beauty" that is an integral part of my taste today.

Once my mother had finished her assessment and checked for identification marks (on the dolls, usually an imprint on the back of the neck; on the bears, a tag on the ear), she would begin the restoration. She worked with a small network of women across London who each specialized in some aspect of a doll's wardrobe. One woman, a homeworker, made beautiful straw hats and lacy bonnets, always using authentic trim and buttons. Another made charming miniature leather shoes.

Victorian dolls' hat and
knitted booties

My mother sold the restored dolls and teddy bears from a booth in Camden Passage in north London. She would arrive, unwrap her prized possessions and display them proudly on the shelves that lined her booth. Her turnover was fast, for her work was appreciated, and she opened only two days a week. Her experience and taste told her just how much to restore something without overdoing it. She knew when a tear or a hole added to the charm of a doll or a bear. Most of her customers were women, and they would come from all over the world to buy from her. Often their children were grown, or they had given their own dolls away as children and were now seeking to replace them. Or they would come just to talk about their childhoods and to recount proudly how they had, in childhood, saved their dolls from destructive brothers. Men would sometimes stop by, too, for the teddy bears.

Money would eventually change hands, but almost as an afterthought. The ritual was infinitely more important than the money or the possession. There was an appreciation of history, an exchange of experiences, and the willingness to listen to someone else's story—moments that can never exist when buying from today's shopping malls and mail-order catalogues.

And then there was my father and his second-hand rare-book business. Originally led into the world of books by his appreciation for the written word, he also respected the fine leather bindings and admired the plates of the great illustrators Arthur Rackham, Kate Greenway, and Beatrix Potter. But what excited him most was the search. With speed and determination he would seek and ultimately find what he was searching for. I have vivid memories of trying to keep up with him, of how quickly his legs would carry him through crowds and the aisles of product.

As with my mother, the conversation that came with the exchange was of great interest and pleasure to him. I was in awe of his ability to see so quickly, to recognize treasures in the blink of an eye. I thank my father for passing that on to me.

My Saturdays were spent hanging around the antique market. I remember the rolling of the eyes when the truth was stretched, the dramas of everyday business, the support when something was stolen or broken, and the sadness when a neighbor shut down.

The eccentric flea-market habits I observed: the crumpled envelopes containing money with small sums scribbled on them, stuffed into pockets and bags. Every vendor seemed to have several of them. As a child I never understood this habit and was irritated by them. Now, of course, I have an envelope in my back pocket with "purchasing money" written on it, another in my bag for "money not to spend but to borrow if need be," and yet another stashed away with "money I may owe someone." As did my mentors, I keep careful track of the contents of these envelopes.

I remember occasionally being left in charge at my mother's booth while she would take a break and the excitement of wheeling and dealing in her absence. On one occasion I bought a doll from somebody who came by when I was in charge—it was, of course, an imperfect, cracked, boy doll.

The seed was planted in me from an early age. I learned to appreciate vintage and history, I came to possess a clarity of mind when identifying my quarry and a quick decisiveness when capturing my finds, and I honed an ability to know what to restore and, more important, what to leave alone.

And so, for me, visiting flea markets and antique malls is like going home.

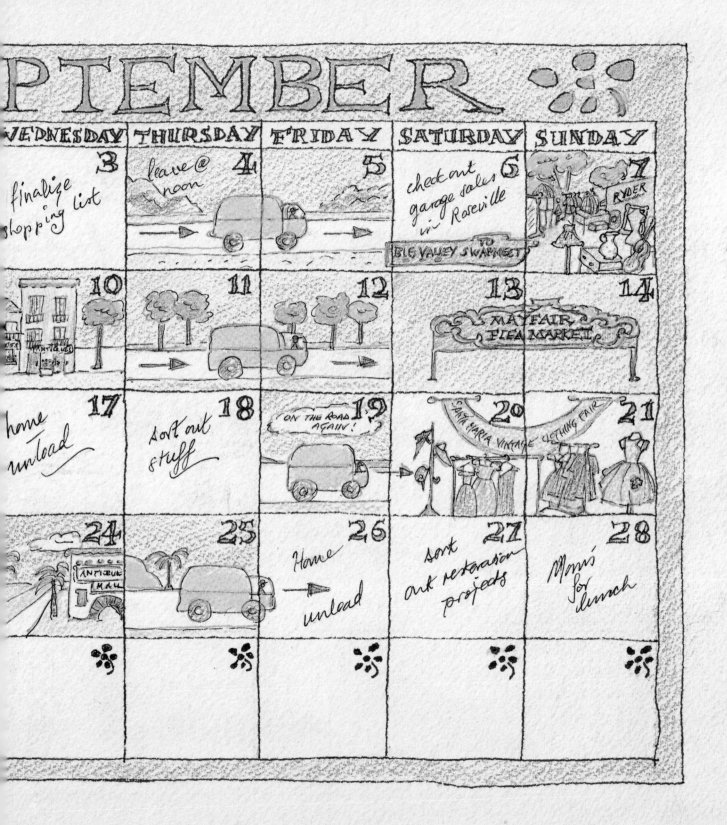

FLEA

MARKETS & RESTORATION

chapter 1

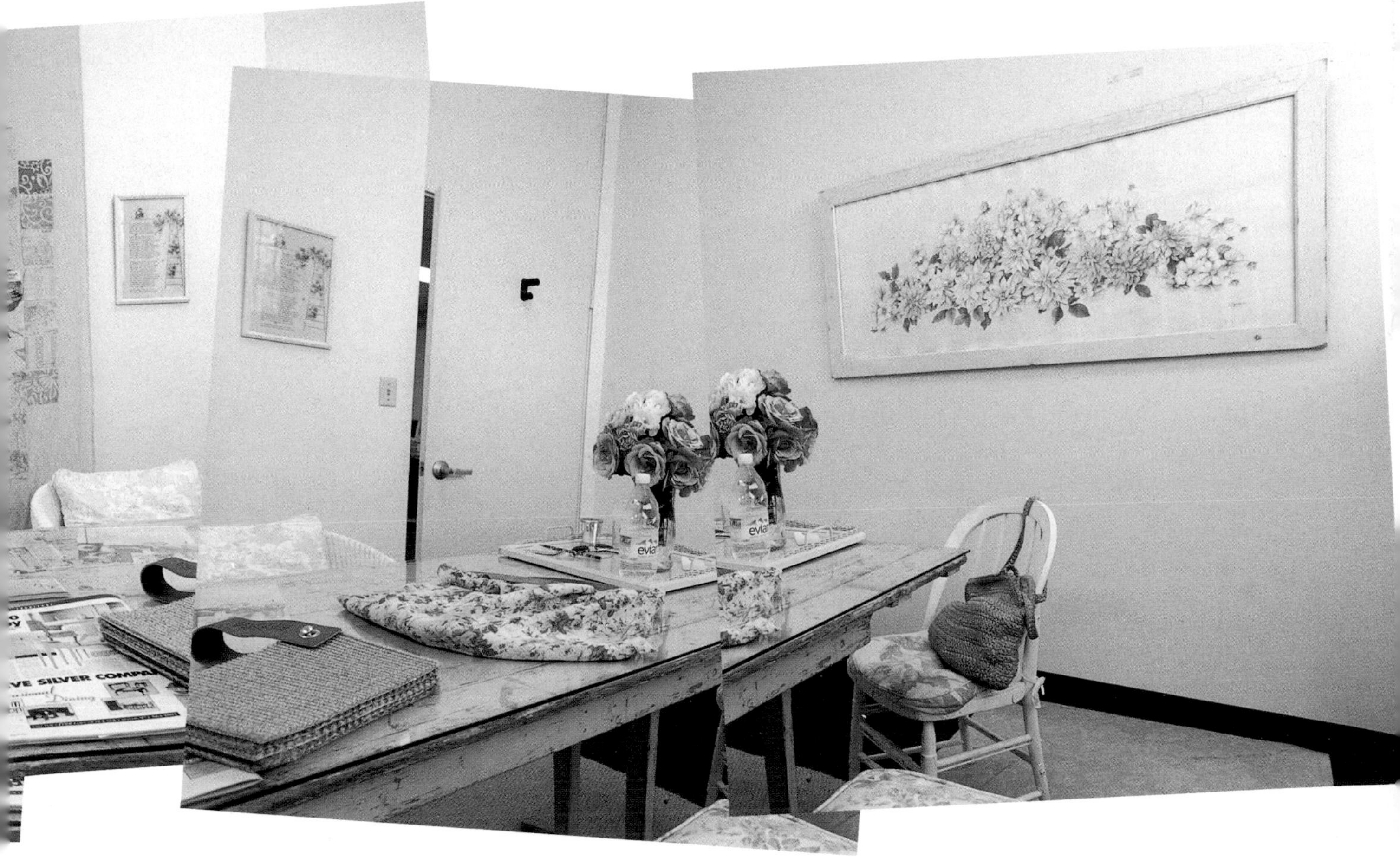

FLEA MARKETS AND RESTORATION

What to look for and how to decorate with secondhand treasures

Celadon greens, mint and seafoam; dusty roses; ivories, creams, and faded grays; a touch of pale sky blue; crisp, clean whites. Worn damask, faded velvets, tea-stained florals, washed-out cotton prints, tattered lace, monogrammed linen. Worn grandeur, the incomplete, the neglected, the crumbling, the cracked, the mismatched, the wrinkled. Ruffles, gathers, tucking; scuffed, chipped, imperfect; scratched moldings, discarded beauty, peeling paint. This is Shabby Chic—the colors that make up my palette; the qualities that suggest things inherited rather than bought.

After color and character, I look for workmanship. Usually this means work done by hand: in furniture, tongue-in-groove joints; in dresses, hand stitching. My own taste centers on faded elegance, muted colors, worn moldings, honestly-come-by crackled paints.

I follow one more basic rule: Function. Everything I buy is functional (although often its function is one other than for which it was originally intended), and is bought with a thought of how it will blend with what I already own. I don't collect anything— no tchotchkes! It is important that you develop and define your taste. You may be fortunate enough to be born with a good "eye," but taste requires work, time, and experience. You will develop it by looking and paying attention, and by making a few mistakes.

It is early morning—a little after five o'clock—and I am arriving at a flea market. The vendors are still unpacking their wares. A glimpse of dusty celadon green catches my eye and I pause.

The green is the pottery base of a table lamp. The shade is exquisite. The cream silk has yellowed, and a ruffle of mottled fabric—the original cream alternating with infinitely faded pink—has worn though in places, although some tiny bows remain, peeking through the tattered tucks. The lining is split in many places but I don't care: I buy it. Shades with this detailing are among my favorite flea-market finds, but I am not put off by an unattractive or hopelessly damaged shade on a good base. A plain parchment or white linen shade, although in a completely different way, can bring the lamp back to life. (Although, however new or functional the wiring seems, I always have lamps professionally rewired.) In addition to table lamps, the stall contains sconces and chandeliers. Immediately my eye is drawn to a metal wall sconce, painted cream with green leaves and buds which add touches of pink. My palette! I am not discouraged by the worn metal or the chipped paint. The sconce would not be difficult to restore, but I like its shabby elegance and will probably leave it as it is. In addition to the rewiring I will need to replace the candle sleeves—not a difficult job. I buy it and ask the price of an alabaster table lamp but decide, after adding in the cost of rewiring, that it is too expensive. Nevertheless, I make a note of the lamp and its location. There are many interested customers at the stall, so I am in a weak bargaining position. If, when I return for the sconce at the end of my day, the lamp hasn't sold, the dealer may prefer to reduce the price rather than pack it up and take it home.

(previous spread)
My office. A site of both creativity and stress—no business functions without endless decision-making. It is important that my office be both practical and aesthetically pleasing. Clearly visible are reminders of Shabby Chic, aesthetically and functionally. A view of my past collections inspires my future projects. Glass covers a rough picnic table and allows photographs, sketches, and swatches to be displayed. Glass-fronted cabinets allow for easy viewing of fabrics. Repainted flea-market wicker chairs have some of my fabric designs tossed to them to test response. My full palette is spread throughout the room.

10

Before I leave I start my list, jotting down the purchases, how much they cost, and the location of the vendor who sold them. By the time I am finished, especially if I have had a successful day, I may have become a little vague about where I bought things. I move on.

Metal furniture is next; I am taken with the detailing on the weathered leg of a wrought-iron garden table. Its glass top is missing, but I am not deterred. The veined leaves are intricate and I can see that the piece is old. Peeling white paint reveals the scuffed iron beneath. I pick my way deeper into the booth where I see dilapidated bed frames, and I am drawn by the patina where the ivory paint has worn through to show traces of an earlier green. Swiftly I buy the bedstead, the garden table, and two similar but not matching iron garden chairs. The chairs will be delightful when I have painted them ivory and given them mushy down cushions covered in faded floral chintz—perhaps of autumnal pale blue, gray, and washed-out green leaves.

Over the years my eye has developed the ability to "edit" out irrelevant merchandise at flea markets. I no longer register the old lawn mowers or the fifties plastic furniture, so the next time I pause it is at a stall that always has a large selection of fabric.

I rarely leave this vendor empty-handed. It is here—among the worn velvets, the ruffled tablecloths, the tattered lace, the white-on-white bedspreads—that I will find the chintz for my newly purchased garden chairs. The chintz is just the way I like it: washed so many times that no trace of the glaze remains. I also buy a length of hand-blocked cotton print—rose on white with a green so faded it is almost gray. Not only are many of the fabrics this dealer offers not available new, but this is by far the most economical way of buying linen, tablecloths, and fabric to cover furniture and cushions. Old-fashioned embroidered or lacy hand towels make lovely presents, both traditional and romantic.

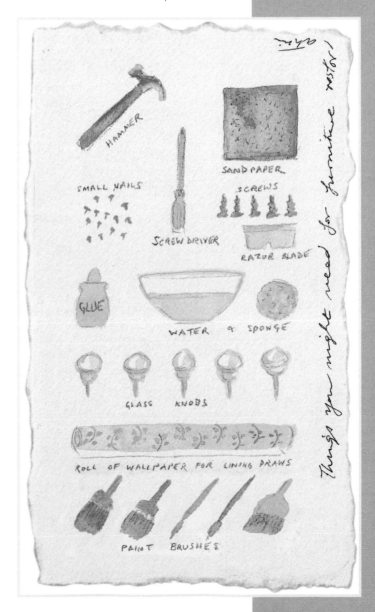

HAMMER

SAND PAPER

SMALL NAILS

SCREWS

SCREW DRIVER

RAZOR BLADE

GLUE

WATER & SPONGE

GLASS KNOBS

ROLL OF WALLPAPER FOR LINING DRAWS

PAINT BRUSHES

Things you might need for furniture restorers!

1

2

3

4

5

6

7

8

9

10

11

12

13

14

15

16

17

18

Loving Greetings

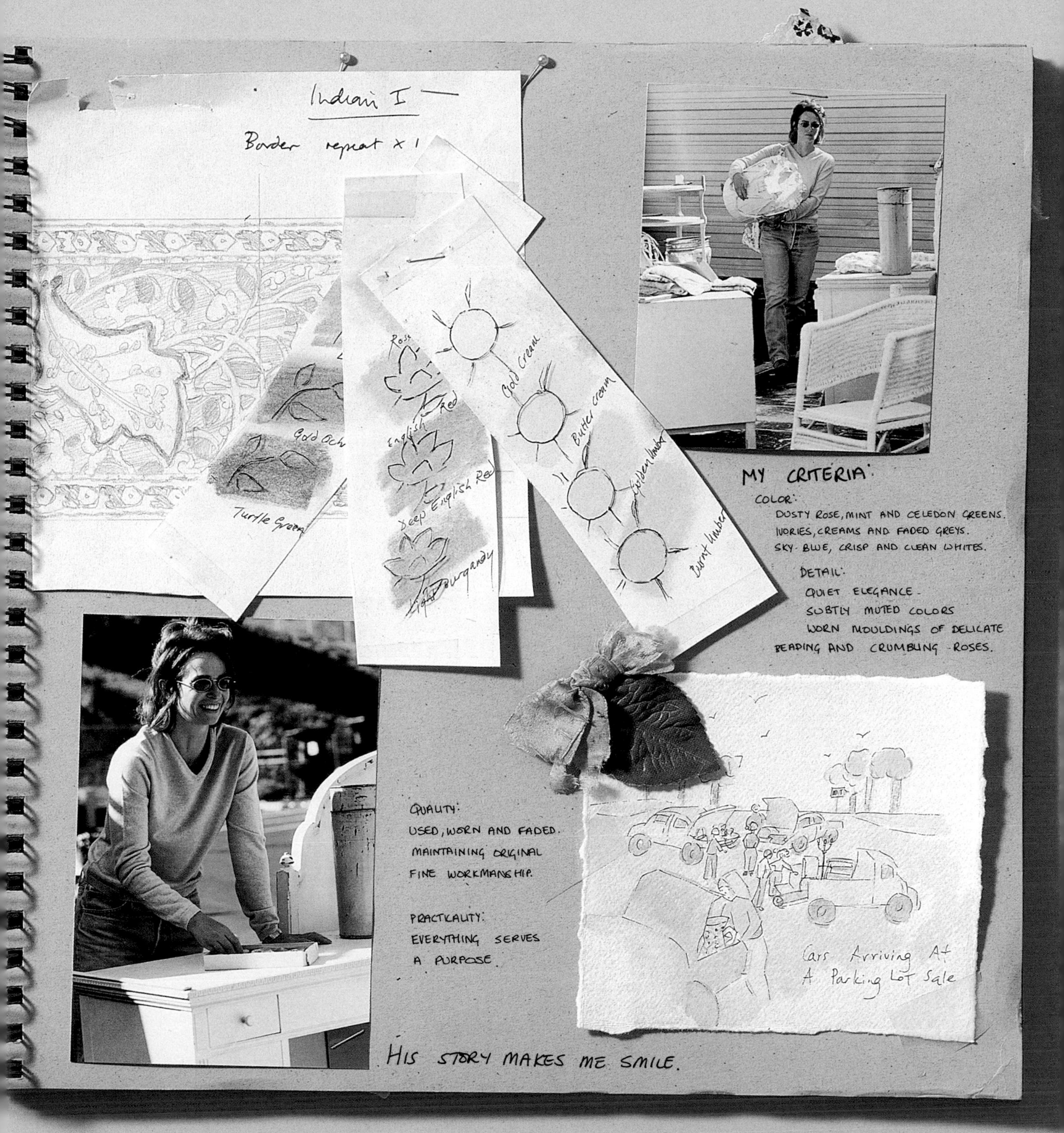

Indian I—

Border repeat × 1

Turtle Green

Gold Ochre

Ross

English Red

Deep English Red

Light Burgundy

Gold Cream

Butter Cream

Golden Umber

Burnt Umber

MY CRITERIA:

COLOR:
DUSTY ROSE, MINT AND CELEDON GREENS.
IVORIES, CREAMS AND FADED GREYS.
SKY-BLUE, CRISP AND CLEAN WHITES.

DETAIL:
QUIET ELEGANCE.
SUBTLY MUTED COLORS
WORN MOULDINGS OF DELICATE
READING AND CRUMBLING ROSES.

QUALITY:
USED, WORN AND FADED.
MAINTAINING ORIGINAL
FINE WORKMANSHIP.

PRACTICALITY:
EVERYTHING SERVES
A PURPOSE.

Cars Arriving At
A Parking Lot Sale

HIS STORY MAKES ME SMILE.

My next stop is at a booth where, at first glance, I am much less likely to find treasure. Here I spot a far-from-lovely "built-in" salvaged from a demolition or a renovation. Unlike my iron furniture or crumpled fabric, this piece has no intrinsic beauty. Since it was not originally a real piece of furniture but merely shelving and storage built into an existing space, it lacks either fine workmanship or attractive materials. Either way, I have a plan for it, one that will require some work, but work that anyone can do with a little time and money. To me, this is what flea markets are about. In my mind, the linoleum that tops the piece and the contact paper that lines the shelves have already been stripped away. I am mentally sanding the wood, adding a coat of thick, pale cream oil-based paint, and replacing the metal knobs with glass ones from my collection.

I continue on and stop in front of a box of old doorknobs. I rummage through them and choose a selection: glass knobs, large enough for the door to a room; similar small replacements for the built-in; six plain white ceramic drawer pulls and a dozen with pastel floral designs. Although several of them match, they are not a set, but they are approximately the same size and I think some of them will mix nicely with others I have in a box at home. Uniformity and perfection are not what I am looking for. Although I never buy anything that does not perform some function, I am always on the lookout for old and aesthetically pleasing knobs and hard-

ware, such as latches and hinges—even if I have no immediate use for them, I know I will eventually need them and be grateful to have a selection on hand. I pay for the drawer pulls and doorknobs and arrange to pick them up later. I try not to weigh myself down with my purchases, especially at the beginning of the day. Twenty doorknobs could feel very heavy by midmorning.

Moving on, I skip several stalls. The tables loaded with tube socks and batteries are easy to ignore, but I also pass up a booth where a less experienced decorator might pause. This vendor specializes in faux finish—in other words, he hamfistedly takes what might have been viable pieces of furniture and paints them to look timeworn, adding a few dollars to what the original piece would have cost. These booths should not be confused with what I call "organized booths"—where the merchandise has been sorted but not "dickered" with. It is much easier to see and evaluate pieces at organized booths, and they are useful places for a first-time flea-market shopper to develop his eye.

I make a regular stop at the vendor who sells wicker furniture. First I lift a peeling, weather-beaten chair to make sure it weighs as much as I think it should. Old wicker furniture is not as light as less substantial modern copies. At the same time I verify that the wicker is woven tightly into place—if it starts to unravel it becomes rather like a run in a stocking. Next I check to see how sturdy the legs and structure are. As a general rule, I am not interested in furniture that is not structurally sound; a rickety chair or wobbly table is not functional, and I buy nothing that cannot actually be used. Some of the pieces are damaged, and I calculate the cost of repairing each. Repairing wicker is never cheap; it is a question of what the restored piece is worth to me.

I see two other pieces I like, a scuffed wooden rocking chair with woven cane panels in the back and arms—it will receive a well-stuffed cushion wrapped in a vintage tablecloth when I have finished with it—and a superficially damaged low table, stiff with cracked cream paint.

No. 4 venetian ornamental frame — any size to order

rustic pattern ornamental oval frame — any width size to order

oval ornamental frame — catalogue No. 950½ — white or gold — any size made to order

Cat. N° 3027
2" × 5⅛"

Nº 3304

diameter 2⅛"

Nº 3051

2⅜" × 2⅞"

Cat. N° 952 — for gilding

square & oval ornamental frames & embossed wood appliques — miscellaneous

15

Although at first glance this salvaged built-in might seem like it needs professional restoration, the tasks at hand are actually rather simple. (Mark first has to gather his strength and his thoughts).

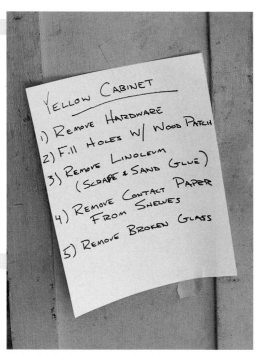

Yellow Cabinet
1) Remove Hardware
2) F.11 Holes w/ Wood Patch
3) Remove Linoleum (Scrape & Sand (glue))
4) Remove Contact Paper From Shelves
5) Remove Broken Glass

Remove the linoleum (linoleum is a common material to be dealt with in these old built-ins). Peeling, picking, and patience are the tools needed here. Occasionally some of the original top may become vulnerable and bruised. You can glue down the loose ends and lightly sand them to blend the surfaces together. The final coat of paint should act as reinforcement.

A simple checklist is created. The contact paper is the first to be removed, by just peeling.

If for any reason the glass breaks, remove it carefully. Take exact measurements for a new piece of glass (the thickness depends on the piece), then tack into place with small nails called brads. Before the paint is applied, a thorough cleaning and light sanding is required to remove any loose bits of dust, dirt, or grime. Tape the edge of the glass with masking tape before painting the wood trim. Use primer first to make way for one or two coats of semigloss paint. You can paint the inside and the outside the same color. I usually paint over everything—even the hardware. (Just make sure, once the hardware is dry, you loosen any piece that may have become stuck or jammed.) In the event that some paint lands up on the glass, wait until it dries and scrape it off with a razor blade.

Now completed this built-in finds its home holding endless bits in my daughter's room.

This green wood table was a find at Bountiful. Twelve feet long, it is perfect for a conference. Placing glass on the top creates a smooth writing surface and allows for displaying photos. A wicker chair gets tested with some of my fabric designs.

I use this metal desk lamp for additional light—it helps me forget the yucky overhead fluorescent light that came with my office.

A finishing palm sander is used mainly for smoothing surfaces. Use it to lightly skim the top off a painted piece for a bit of distressing, or to smooth wood putty. It allows for more control than the circular sander that would be used for a more drastic task, such as totally stripping off paint from a piece of furniture.

A wonderful mercantile cabinet among the patio furniture stands proudly. It is perfect for a kitchen or an office. With such an expanse of white wood, some glass draw pulls in place of metal handles would offer a sparkle.

White Cabinet

Removed Metal Handles

Patched Holes

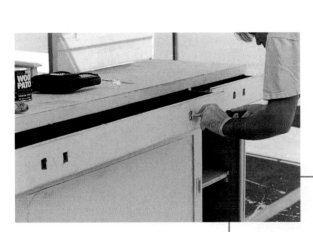

The first step would be to remove the holes left by the metal handles. The smoother the application of putty the less sanding is necessary. Two hours of hardening will be required before light sanding is done to smooth out the edges. Drill holes for new glass draw pulls; always make the hole a little smaller than the screw to give some torque. Finally, some simple dusting and cleaning will transform this piece. In this case, no painting was ever needed.

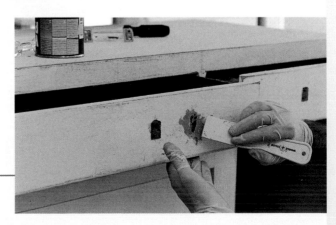

If you find yourself wanting to distress the paint from a piece of furniture, choose your spots intelligently: where there would be natural wear and tear, around draw pulls or knobs, edges, and on top of surfaces.

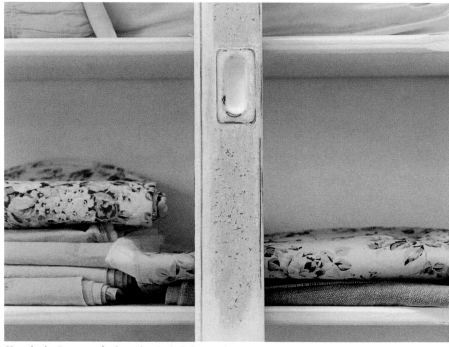

How lucky I was to find, with a little light sanding, my green under the white.

A filing cabinet is always a nice discovery. Check the ease of the drawer sliding. Large glass knobs will enhance this piece nicely.

Both are structurally sound, so I buy them; the rocker will require a cleaning to make it as good as—or, better than—new. The table does not warrant the expenditure of money or labor; I will cover the top with a piece of washed-out cotton print cloth and a sheet of glass. I pay for them, and as I walk away I make a mental note of some slightly more damaged pieces. One, at least, deserves further consideration.

By now I am thirsty and a little tired. I have had a successful morning and I pause for a drink. Because flea-market food tends to be neither very appetizing nor particularly nutritious, I have brought a sandwich and some fruit from home. While I take my break, I chat with a few vendors I know.

This cabinet, now with glass drawer handles, is the perfect solution to hold all my bits in my office.

This knobless chest of draws had the perfect finish when I found it at the Santa Monica Flea Market. The blue trim on the inside of the draws created a lovely accent waiting to be lined.

Lining the drawers with vintage wallpaper is a wonderful way to complete restoration of a piece.

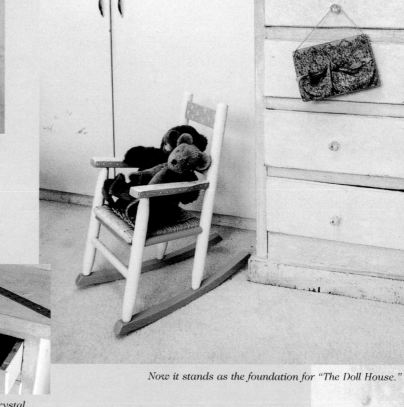

Now it stands as the foundation for "The Doll House."

The final addition was to add crystal knobs. The unusual proportion of this piece made it appropriate for placement in a tight spot.

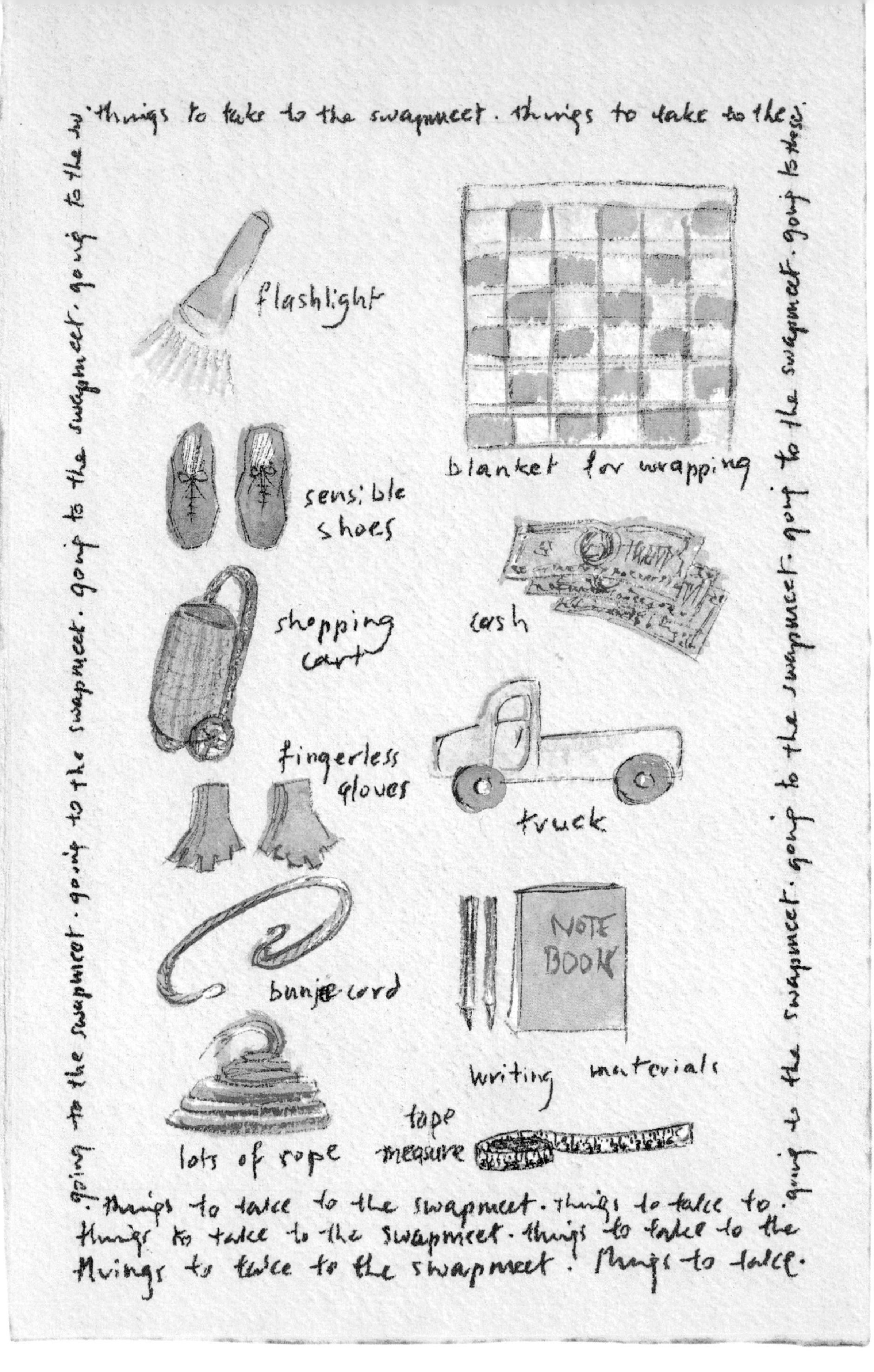
things to take to the swapmeet. things to take to the
going to the swapmeet. going to the swapmeet. going to the swapmeet. going to the
going to the swapmeet. going to the swapmeet. going to the swapmeet. going to the
flashlight
blanket for wrapping
sensible shoes
shopping cart
cash
fingerless gloves
truck
NOTE BOOK
bunje cord
writing materials
tape measure
lots of rope
things to take to the swapmeet. things to take to.
things to take to the swapmeet. things to take to the
things to take to the swapmeet. things to take.

I ask one about floral oil paintings—I always have a need for them and love the way the dark cracks in the old oil paint contrasts with the delicate blues, pinks, and greens of the flowers. This dealer doesn't have any but promises to keep an eye open for some. I enjoy these moments of conversation at markets.

This is a good moment to go over my list of what I have bought and what I have spent. This is largely a cash business, so I keep careful accounts. Although I keep one eye open for that once-in-a-lifetime buy, making a fortune from some treasure that only I recognize is a very long shot. Instead, I try to buy items that please my eye for a fair price.

Dishes in blues, greens, deep pinks; sparkling glassware and vases of china or colored and clear glass, dazzling in the sunlight. The glint from the small blue-ribboned bundles of silver spoons. Decorations—the approach makes me think of fairyland. I take some time to adjust my eye to visualize the uses for the variety of wares in front of me. (Remember, everything must be functional.) I am charmed by a plate with a lavender pattern. I'm not sure I'd want to eat off a lavender plate, but it seems to me that with three or four cakes of pink soap on it, it would look very good in my white-tiled bathroom. I buy it, because it is far from expensive and I have never seen one quite like it.

Happily in possession of the lavender plate, I turn my attention to the glassware. There is still plenty of pressed inexpensive glass—clear, pink, green, amber—in different qualities and weights for sale at flea markets. I buy a selection of pressed glass bowls, which will have many uses—salads, fruit, desserts—and a cream-colored jug with a muted pastel floral design on the front, probably from the late twenties or early thirties. It will be useful either as a serving piece, or, as I visualize it now, full of flowers. It would also make a wonderful present. If a piece of china appeals to me I don't mind if it is slightly chipped—there are many chips and imperfections in this particular fairyland—and a coat of nail polish covers a multitude of defects. There is also a large box of inexpensive decorations. I never waste money on new, store-bought wrapping or ribbon. During the year I pick up a variety of silk flowers, Christmas decorations, and small beaded brooches and store my decorations in a miniature chest of drawers made of stiff cardboard and covered with vintage wallpaper, originally intended for lingerie. My bits and bobs are filed away in the various drawers, and when I need to wrap a present I can easily choose the decoration that seems most fitting for the recipient and the gift.

I tore this myself accidentally— although the painting is pretty, it doesn't warrant expensive restoration. Simple linen tape applied to the back and a light smudging of paint over the tear is an acceptable repair that adds character.

The ultimate use of this table would dictate the amount of restoration needed. Although its dainty legs are quite stable, the condition of the top is the extreme side of shabby, but usable, if used ornamentally. However, the same table could become much more functional with the simple addition of a piece of glass and fabric.

I found this rocking chair on a shopping trip to Summerland Antiques. Instantly in my mind I replaced the seat cushion cover.

One of the most comfortable chairs I have ever sat in is this rocker. In its original form it lacked luster, but the simple task of wrapping an old but fresh white tablecloth around its seat elevated it to another class.

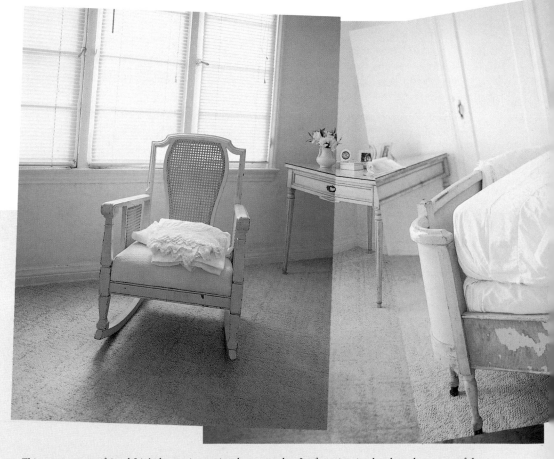

This room at my friend Liz's house is as simple as can be. Its function is clearly to be a peaceful and restful sanctuary. All day a magical light dances on the few, carefully chosen pieces in the room, making whites and creams look cool and rich. The patina on the aged wood of this flea-market–found vintage bed softly complements the crisp and clean white bedding. The bed cover folds comfortably over the rounded gap at the end of the bed.

Vintage beds can be a wonderful focal point in a bedroom. There are certain characteristics to look for when purchasing an old bed.

1. Make sure side rails are included. You can always get new ones made, but it detracts from the authenticity and additional cost has to be considered.

2. Old beds often do not match the standard sizes of today:

Twin: 38 x 75
Full: 53 x 75
Queen: 60 x 80
King: 72 x 84

Custom mattresses can be made, but they can get expensive.

3. It is vital that the bed be thoroughly cleaned, followed by a light sanding to remove any loose paint chips and rust.

Setting off toward vintage clothing, I keep one eye open for frames, particularly if they are oversized (larger than 3' x 4'). I love the theatricality of a huge mirror, the glass mottled enough to add character, but not so mottled that it isn't useful. I often paint the carved wood or gold frame white, because I like the effect to be dramatic, not overwhelming.

Next I visit a booth that sells beds, bedside tables, sofas, chairs, and armoires. None of the beds have the level of carved floral detail that I look for—or the patina, the layering of paint—but I see two armoires I could use. One has lovely little carvings of roses. On the other the molding is incomplete, but there are beautiful details of worn-away wreaths, angels, and a floral design. I like this piece best, partly because the moldings are so worn—if they looked newer they would be too overwhelming. I think the first armoire is over-priced; I make an offer, which the vendor declines, but after a little negotiating I buy the second and continue on my way.

The vintage clothing booths are clustered together. Many of my jeans and cashmere cardigans come from the flea market, and I often buy my dress-up or special-occasion clothes at vintage clothing and textile shows. The silks and satins, the embroideries, and bias-cut dresses reflect a level of detail and workmanship only found today in couture collections.

It is now time for me to collect my purchases. It has been a rewarding and productive morning. Over the years I have learned to go through a flea market quickly, and because most of my visits take place on my Sunday off after a working week, I try to be finished by noon. The flea markets themselves usually close at about three o'clock. I almost always find something. Although occasionally I return home empty-handed, I never feel the day has been wasted, having learned something, enjoyed talking to vendors and friends, and further defined what I like, what is aesthetically important and meaningful to me.

Tired and pleased, I have already collected some of my goods when I catch a glimpse from across two aisles of something cream with a touch of dusty pink. I feel that familiar flutter and, quickening my pace, cut across toward the stall where the possible treasure lies. This reaction, less of a skill than a time-learned instinct, has served me well.

Whether I had an existing need for these fabulous antique French frames, or not, I would always snap them up. Priceless and beautifully detailed moldings in a variety of conditions are a typical example of decayed elegance. Adding mirrors and making sure the frames are bracketed for safe hanging are simple restoration steps to a wonderful piece. Here one sits casually on Liz's floor.

There are many venues where you can look for antiques and second-hand treasures. My favorites are flea markets and antiques malls.

MISCELLANEOUS SIDEBAR INFORMATION

Washing Porcelain

PUT A TOWEL IN THE BOTTOM OF THE SINK AND FILL WITH WARM WATER, NOT HOT, AND A MILD DISHWISHING SOAP TO WHICH YOU HAVE ADDED ONE OUNCE OF CLEAR AMMONIA. SOAK AND RINSE WELL.

Washing Glass

TO CLEAN GLASS, SOAK IN A SOLUTION OF WARM WATER MIXED WITH 1/4 CUP OF CLEAR AMMONIA. RINSE WELL AND DRY CAREFULLY. AS WITH PORCELAIN, IT IS A GOOD IDEA TO PLACE A TOWEL IN THE BOTTOM OF THE SINK FIRST WHEN WASHING DELICATE CRYSTAL. SOME OLD GLASS BOTTLES CAN BECOME CLOUDED OR DISCOLORED AND CAN BE TREATED BY SOAKING IN A MIXTURE OF ONE CUP OF AMMONIA AND FOUR CUPS OF WARM WATER. ANOTHER METHOD IS TO MIX SAND WITH DENATURED ALCOHOL AND SWIRL IT AROUND IN THE CONTAINER UNTIL IT LOOKS CLEAR. WHITE VINEGAR AND WATER MAY BE USED TO SOAK OFF SEDIMENT THAT MAY HAVE ADHERED TO THE INSIDE OF A GLASS CONTAINER. FILL CONTAINER WITH THIS MIXTURE AND LEAVE TO SOAK FOR A FEW DAYS.

Cleaning Brass

CUT A LEMON IN HALF, DIP IT IN SALT AND USE TO SCRUB BRASS. THIS WORKS WELL FOR COPPER TOO. YOU CAN ALSO MAKE A SCRUBBING PASTE FROM ONE TABLESPOON EACH OF SALT, FLOUR, AND WHITE VINEGAR. RUB ON AND BE SURE TO RINSE WELL IN EITHER METHOD.

Removing Rust

USE A WIRE BRUSH TO REMOVE LOOSE RUST FROM WROUGHT IRON FURNITURE AND ORNAMENTS. THEN SAND LIGHTLY OR RUB WITH SOME FINE STEEL WOOL DIPPED IN KEROSENE. AFTER THE KEROSENE HAS DRIED, THE PIECE CAN BE PAINTED WITH AN OUTDOOR PAINT.

Removing Beverage Rings

TO TRY AND REMOVE THOSE WHITE RINGS LEFT ON WOOD SURFACES FORMED BY CONDENSATION FROM DRINKING GLASSES, TRY MIXING UP A PASTE OF CIGARETTE ASH WITH SOME BEESWAX FURNITURE PASTE. RUB ON LIGHTLY AND BUFF WITH A DRY SOFT CLOTH. YOU CAN THEN REWAX THE WHOLE SURFACE IF NECESSARY.

Reviving Cane & Wicker

OLD WICKER OR CANE FURNITURE CAN BE HOSED OFF OUTDOORS TO REMOVE LOOSE DUST AND GRIME. IF NEEDED, IT CAN BE SCRUBBED WITH A SMALL BRUSH DIPPED IN DISHWASHING LIQUID AND WATER. RINSE AND SUN DRY. IT CAN BE VARNISHED IN A MATTE TO GLOSS FINISH OR PAINTED WITH A THIN COAT OF GOOD QUALITY PAINT. FOR SAGGING WOVEN CANE SEATS, COMPLETELY SOAK THE CANING WITH HOT WATER AND LEAVE TO TIGHTEN AND DRY IN THE SUN.

Dying Unfinished Wood

LIGHTLY SAND THE BARE WOOD ITEM AND CAREFULLY DUST OFF. APPLY A SOLUTION OF LIQUID 'RIT' DYE WITH A SPONGE IN CIRCULAR MOTIONS. LET DRY COMPLETELY. THE COLOR WILL BE LIGHTER WHEN DRY, SO REPEAT THE APPLICATION OF DYE TO OBTAIN A RICHER COLOR. YOU MAY WISH TO SEAL THE FINISH WITH A COAT OF VARNISH.

FLEA MARKETS

I find flea markets the most fun and the most challenging places to hunt and gather, because they offer the widest variety of merchandise and are the greatest test of skill, once you understand a few basics and don't take any of it too seriously.

There are hundreds, probably thousands, of flea markets across the country. I've listed my favorites in the back of this book, along with information on how to obtain lists of flea markets in your area. Some are held monthly, others less regularly. If they take place more than once a month, I usually don't bother going; vendors don't have time to buy and restock. If you frequent a flea market, you may build relationships with particular vendors, and in time they will be happy to save items of interest to you.

Most vendors price their items with a little negotiating room, but because they work hard and have to put up with moans, groans, and bargaining, I try to decide what an item is worth to me before I ask the best price. It will be my gauge of whether the asking price is fair. In time, gauging a fair price will become second nature to you. Vendors will usually store your purchases if they are cumbersome or if you want to continue shopping empty-handed, but make clear and descriptive notes of where you've left them. Otherwise, when it's time to gather your finds, you may see hundreds of "small green trees by white vans."

Going to some of the larger flea markets (often those that are quarterly or even yearly) takes a little more organization. If your visit will require an overnight stay, make hotel reservations well in advance. If you are very serious and taking a big truck, make sure that the hotel has adequate parking. You may want to take traveler's checks, because many vendors do not accept out-of-town personal checks and are more willing to negotiate in a cash sale.

Because flea markets are held outdoors, consider the weather and be prepared. Comfortable shoes, a lightweight waterproof poncho, and a hat or sun block can be lifesavers. You can find yourself walking miles and miles at flea markets and for the most part in the United States, the only refreshments on hand are hot dogs, coffee, soda, and doughnuts. I bring something a little more healthful and palatable and am always grateful I have done so.

Among the madness and chaos of the flea markets are some stalls with total organization and vision. In this space, the vendor knows what she has and presents it well. You may not uncover hidden treasures, but bargains and uniqueness are still achieved.

Things I Need

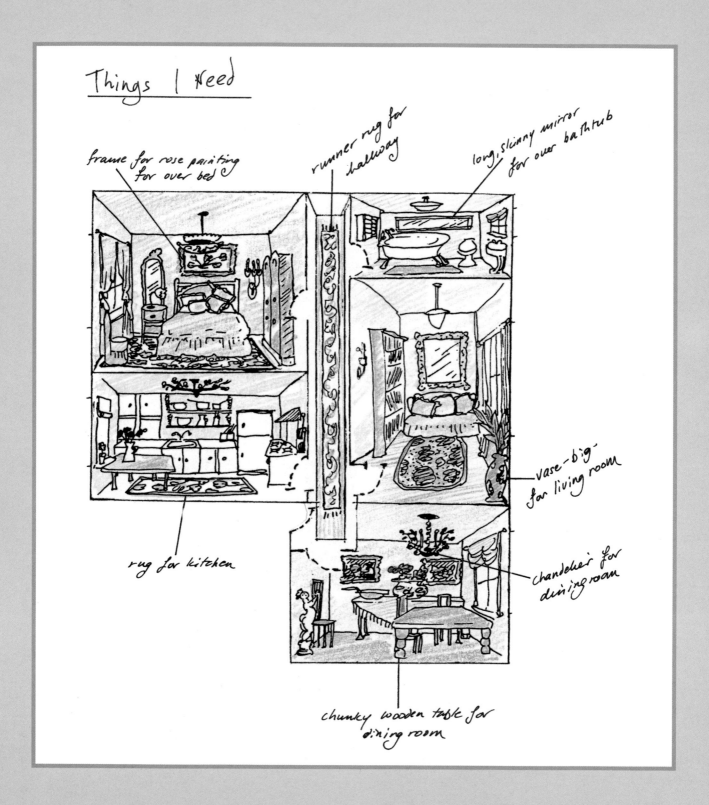

frame for rose painting
for over bed

runner rug for
hallway

long, skinny mirror
for over bathtub

rug for kitchen

vase - big -
for living room

chandelier for
dining room

chunky wooden table for
dining room

The most important lesson I have learned during the years, is to be organized and disciplined both practically and emotionally. Knowing what you need or what you like allows for quick thinking. At a flea market, this is half the battle. Showing interest in an item draws attention to it and attracts competitors. If you ponder or dither—you may lose out. The time to buy something is when you first see it. If the price is more than you are prepared to pay, holding out until the end of the day when the vendor may be more amenable to negotiation—is also an option. But it is a risk, too. Being prepared with specifics like measurements and fabric swatches is helpful. Before I understood this, many times I brought home something too large to fit through my door or too small to be of any use.

You will make mistakes; I still do. It happens. I accept my imperfections.

Once I've gathered items, I amaze myself at how loyally I re-create my palette. The little pink mirror's frame will need a small touch-up; all else will need just soap and water.

(opposite page)
Proof to me once again that making the rounds of the antique malls is worth it. After pacing and pacing through aisles of dark oak and fifties Formica furniture, I found this exquisite sideboard secretly tucked away. The faded green coloring and painted pink flowers captured my gaze. The dining space at my friend Liz's home is now complete.

An Antique Mall

ANTIQUE MALLS

I think antique malls are the best-kept secret and most underrated source of antiques and secondhand goodies.

Nearly every town in the country has an antiques shopping area; the local chamber of commerce can usually tell you where it is located. Within that area there are antiques malls—large buildings, sometimes old warehouses or old barns, that a group of antiques dealers share.

Prices may be a little higher than at flea markets, but this is not always the case and it is such a civilized way to shop. Parking tends to be convenient. Usually each individual booth is not staffed, but welcoming and cooperative personnel are available to answer questions and help carry goods.

Merchandise is clearly displayed and accessible and I have time to ponder. I rarely feel that an item will be snapped up by somebody else if I don't make up my mind immediately. Some malls will even put things on hold for a few days or offer them on lay-away.

There is usually a 10 percent negotiating margin, although isolated booths within the mall may have their own sales and there significantly larger discounts can be obtained. Most antiques malls will be happy to take checks or credit cards.

As with flea markets, shopping in antiques malls requires imagination and perseverance. I often spend days driving from one mall to another, and I never come home empty-handed.

This very small section of Nina and Lou's compact house is not to be wasted. It serves as a library and office area. The choice of colors for the desk and storage containers cheers what could have been a gloomy corner.

This pink kitchen table did not need much from my imagination. I found it in a store that does a nice job displaying its wares. You may pay a few pennies more but it's worth it.

*One of my finds from Summerland
Antiques. Already I think I know
where some of these will end up.*

At Nina and Lou's this now serves as an end table and cupboard.

ESTATE SALES

Estate sales were originally conducted by auction houses, which would sell off the movable property of an entire estate after the death of the owner. The term was reserved for grand and high-quality antiques and jewelry sold on behalf of the heirs.

Today, however, most "estate sales" take place on the estate, which can be anything from a mansion to a small apartment. In either case, check your local newspaper and neighborhood tree trunks for advertisements. Go early; serious antiques dealers and store owners are usually waiting for the doors to open.

The items for sale may be any kind of personal property, ranging from clothing to appliances to antiques. Goods are usually displayed where they are used with a price tag attached. Prices tend to be fair but not necessarily bargains.

At An Estate Sale

TAG SALES

Tag sales are similar to estate sales. They are usually held in a home, the entire contents of which are offered for sale. Sometimes a professional consultant may conduct the sale and because they are usually paid a commission, it behooves them to get the best price possible. Tag sales run in this fashion tend to be a little more expensive than those organized by the home owner.

Try to go early, but be aware that sometimes professional designers or store owners are notified of a presale: they can buy before the doors are open to the public, and sometimes no goodies are left.

A Yard Sale

YARD & GARAGE SALES

Yard and garage sales have become almost synonymous with moving. They are a means of discarding the unnecessary, and the owners are highly motivated to sell. Household items ranging widely in quality and condition are laid out on the lawn. Sometimes a few neighbors will combine their goods, which can make for a pleasant social gathering. Some even supply doughnuts and drinks.

JUMBLE SALES

Jumble sale is an English term commonly used to describe the sales that take place in a church hall to aid the parish. The term is perfectly descriptive—a cheaply priced jumble of sweaters, china, books, and anything else at hand. It is the buyer's challenge to dig through and find what he can.

A Jumble Sale At The Local Church

Possibility for office

lily's room!

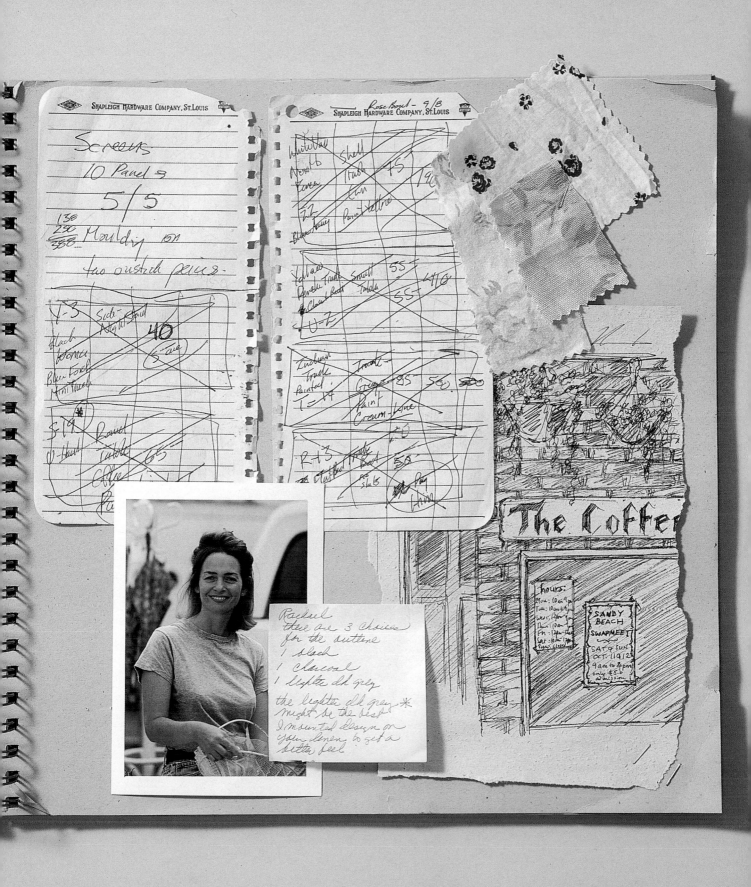

My Palette

A broom.
I love that someone took the time
to paint this a pretty pink.

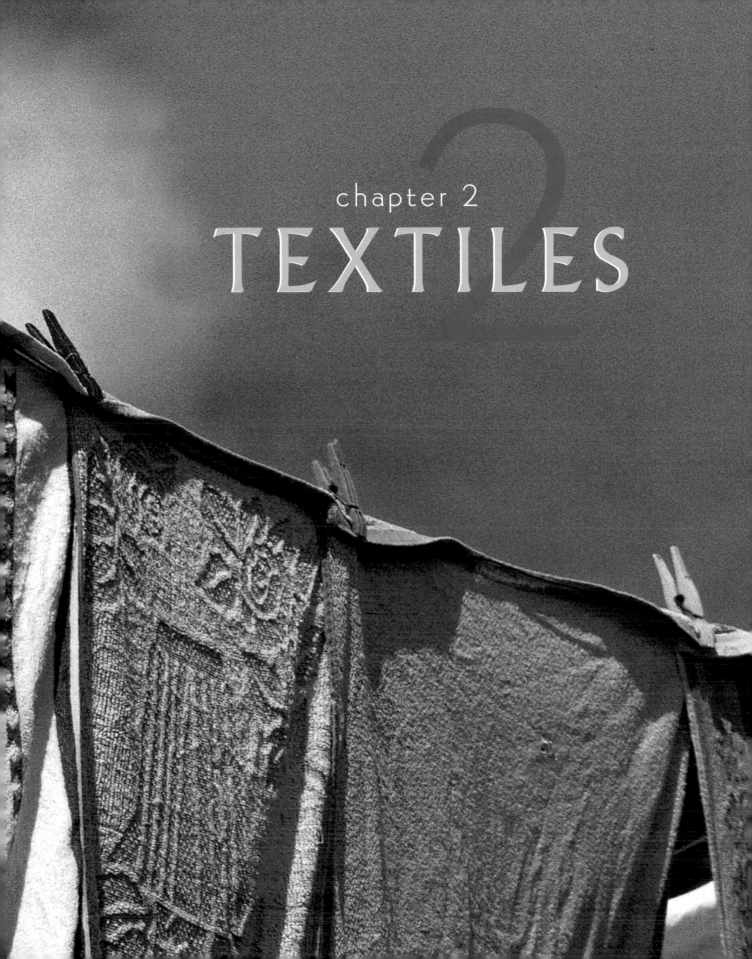

chapter 2
TEXTILES

TEXTILES

Faded Florals and Laundered Linen

Fabrics—scraps of velvet, ribbon, and lace—are among my first flea-market memories. When I was a small child I used to accompany my mother while she searched the booths for remnants of old but fine fabrics. Small quantities, they needed only to be large enough to replace or repair a doll's finery. As soon as I became tall enough to look over the edge of the counter or table, I was fascinated by the drawers full of exquisite colors, delicate silks and satins, creamy laces, and white crochet. My mother would lift a piece and examine it. "This still has a bit of life in it," she'd say.

The textile booths at flea markets or antiques malls still give me pleasure. Whether I am admiring a neat pile of clean, starched, and ironed linen or rummaging though a jumble of tangled cloth, I enjoy this inexpensive and satisfying way of buying fabric.

Sheets, pillowcases, napkins, and hand towels. All are for sale in mass quantities at flea markets. The essential nobility of old, fine, heavy linen only increases with time. Perhaps more than any other item, linen, especially if it bears an embroidered monogram—a bride's initials, the name of a hotel or even that of a railway line—resonates with the past. I look over each piece carefully, worrying less about minor damage than about stains. Small tears can be mended, and for me, a small, exquisite darn, almost as old as the linen itself, only adds to the charm of the piece. But if the dealer has been defeated by a discolored patch, it is unlikely I will do any better when I get it home.

Unlike some flea-market goods that seem a little surprised to find themselves down on their luck—being offered for sale, secondhand—fine old linen remains serene. It was made to last forever; rather than being thrown away, its function changed. A heavy old linen sheet, with its hand stitching and patiently produced embroidery, might have rested for the first few years of its life in a hope chest or bottom drawer, waiting for the girl who had made it to marry and have a home of her own. When the sheet became worn it would have been carefully mended and, later still, when too threadbare to be repaired, it might be cut down for another use—perhaps a sheet for a child's bed—and eventually would end its days as cleaning rags with years of history. Fine linen evokes elegance, luxury, civility, quality, durability, economy—it is the antithesis of everything we abhor about our disposable, use-it-once-and-throw-it-away society.

(previous spread)
Evocative of the fresh smell of newly laundered, line-dried fabric and of the ceremonies surrounding the hand washing, wind drying, and sun bleaching of household cotton and linen. Wash day, although one of hard work, was a ceremony of a kind—a ceremony honoring both the quality of the cloth and the hand that made it.

This upstairs sitting room in the Dern's house is at the end of Andrea's studio. It is often used as a place for Andrea's paintings to dry. Wicker is the obvious choice for this sun-filled and summery room. I love Andrea's work and now sell her floral paintings in my shop.

Whenever I see them, I buy heavy old linen sheets, hand monogrammed, white-on-white, along with sets of shams, pillowcases, and hand towels, none of which need to match one another to make a bedroom or guest bathroom sophisticated and welcoming. If they are lacy or trimmed with tiny, precious, hidden frills, they can be laundered and dressed up to make the perfect bridal shower gift or housewarming present.

I believe that old and beautiful objects are meant to be used, to become part of life. So I buy linen napkins by the dozen, often the former property of hotels or restaurants. They accompany all meals, even of the baked-beans-on-toast variety. Once you accept that linen or cotton napkins do not always need to be ironed, they become an elegant and almost effortless addition to everyday life and cost less than paper napkins. Needless to say, the finer linen and delicate lace I admire is carefully hand washed and gently ironed.

I am always on the lookout for old voile, fine lawn, and linen. I once bought a set of large curtains made out of lovely puckered white cotton inset with panels of handmade lace. I have yards and yards of it folded up. I use it for tablecloths.

The flea market is still an inexpensive place to buy decent-size lengths of fabric. I buy chintz if the colors fit my palette—pale greens, pinks, cream, and white. I like the Victorian floral patterns of chintz but not its shiny quality, so I put it in the washing machine on the hot cycle and after one or two washes it develops a soft, mellow finish—just the way I like it.

This pink sari doubles as my special table-cloth. I also wear it as a skirt. This may seem an unusual choice, but there are no rules about what can and cannot be used for what purpose. The sparkle on this is so lovely.

(opposite page)
Linen napkins and lacy tablecloths are one of those must-have luxuries at my table—constantly in use, with ironing and matching abandoned.

Curtain lengths are an economical way to buy curtains. You have more leeway about the measurements than you may think. If too long, they don't necessarily need to be taken up. Curtains puddling on a wooden floor give a luxurious, sensuous effect. If too short, you can "lengthen" them by using ribbon straps to hang them on the pole. If not quite full enough, they can simply be draped to one side.

But, to apply one of the key tenets of imaginative flea-market thinking, curtain panels need not be used as curtains. Consider them also as a plentiful and inexpensive source of fabric—an old curtain costs a great deal less than a bolt of new material. Would a piece of faded green willow damask enhance your table even if it didn't quite cover every inch of it? If your ultimate use is something smaller than a curtain, imperfections and even stains need not deter you, because you can cut around the unusable bits. Check the panel and measure it to make sure you have enough usable fabric to cover a cushion, window seat, table, or even a smaller window.

If you want to achieve the extravagant effects of puddling but your curtains are not long enough, simply apply loops as Andrea did here to add a few extra inches. Whether you hang antique lace panels, vintage fabrics, or premade curtains, this solution will work nicely.

If you come across a good-quality piece of fabric in which the print, workmanship, ruffles, frills, or pleating appeal to you, but the color is off, don't be discouraged. If the fabric is substantial, such as heavy curtaining, have it professionally dyed. It requires a vat large enough for the fabric to circulate freely and avoid a mottled effect. Your dry cleaner can probably do it for you. Another option for changing the color or shade of fabric is tea-staining. Simple and effective, the instant aging is natural and convincing—antique rather than no longer new; home dyes are also easy to use and come with uncomplicated instructions. To fade material, either bleach it chemically or leave it in the sun; bleach is obviously the faster of the two processes. Not only will the colors become paler, but the patterns will become more subdued and sometimes barely visible. The bleach should be applied carefully, diluted with water, and fabric should always be wet before it is bleached. The texture of fabric can be altered—made lighter and less stiff—by repeated washing and by adding a substantial amount of fabric softener.

Andrea's nook is given respect with one of her paintings. A valence made of tea-towel fabric enhances the window without obscuring light.

A guest towel—I see them all the time at flea markets—is pinned up with thumb tacks and acts as a curtain. Nothing fancy is required, since you rarely need to open the curtain on a bathroom window.

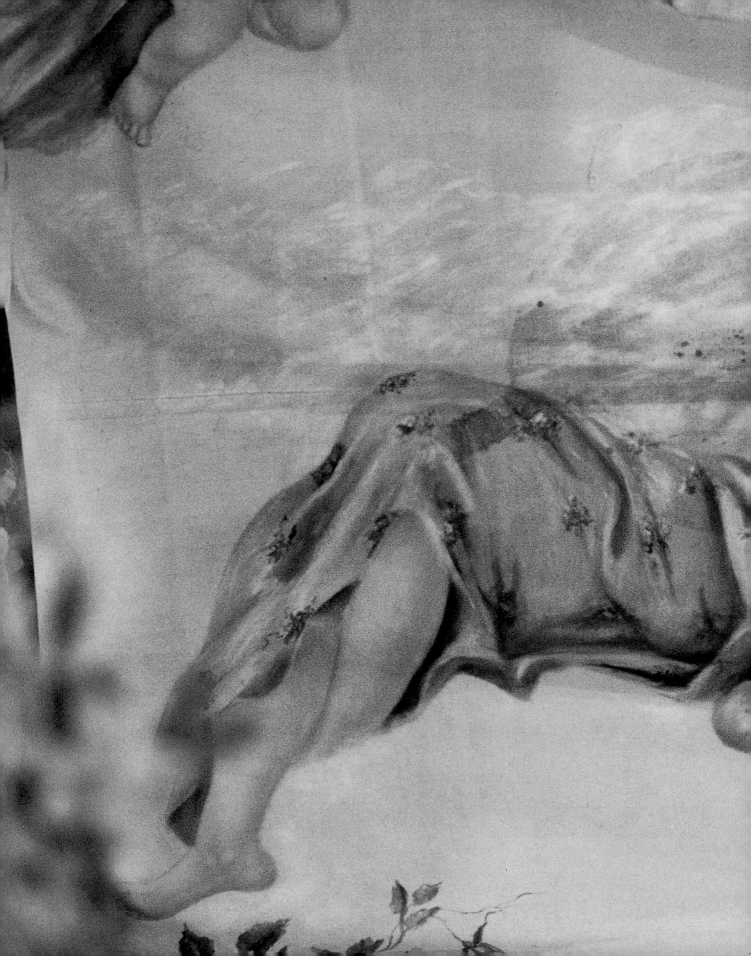

*This hand-painted canvas drop cloth—
probably a remnant from a theatrical
project—would be a casual and whimsical
wall covering (no framing necessary).*

Occasionally I come across the simplest, throwaway piece of fabric, such as an old curtain or pelmet with an exquisite, wonderful ruffling effect. I adore the workmanship and romantic frivolity of these old ruffles, and the piece of fabric becomes a pretty tablecloth with little or no work. Don't forget that layering smaller pieces of material—lace, damask; light material over heavy, heavy over light—on old fabric can cover any amount of imperfections.

SKIRT

TRIPLE LAYER

RUFFLE

A pile of lavender fabric at Lorraine Fogwell's store inspired a theme—throw pillows with an assortment of ruffles.

I was fortunate
enough to buy ten
of these exquisite
chairs at Bountiful.
They are my
favorites, and I
scatter them
throughout my
home. I dress them
with or without
skirt slips depend-
ing on whether I
want a fancy or a
formal look.

Andrea had many pieces of her furniture covered in this costly fabric, anticipating it would fade. Twelve years later it was still crisp and bright so she decided to fade it herself. She tried a couple of different processes on the fabric sleeves and she ended up using bleach and Rit color removal to achieve an instant, faded elegance.

Andrea and Bruce inherited a pair of these unassuming chairs. The simple little slip allowing the legs to show evokes informality. Fabric sleeves on the arms allow for easy, regular washing of the most used part of the chair.

Fortunately most of Andrea's pieces were slipcovered (for the bleaching process); however, in the case of this upholstered ottoman base, eyes rarely see where the fading process couldn't reach.

Although slipcovers to me are the way to renovate any upholstered piece of furniture, endless washing of certain fabrics may cause shrinkage. Andrea helped the length of this skirt by adding some ribbon trim to the hemline.

Andrea had this inexpensive wicker chair floating around. She applied pink paint and a couple of finely ruffled pillows and ended up with a very unique and appealing piece.

Wicker of various qualities is still relatively easy to come by. It's a wonderful casual addition either inside or out. To avoid the expense of reupholstering, laying and tucking an old quilt as Andrea has done complements the wicker perfectly.

Andrea and Bruce inherited this comfy and friendly chair and footstool. Andrea opted not to slipcover this piece, but by simply whitewashing the legs with Gesso, she gave their chair a youthful feel.

Blankets are useful scattered about. This one has nice layering and a lovely texture. A throwaway but subtle detail.

More perhaps than any other commodity, fabric—with a little thought and not much more expense—can dramatically affect the look and atmosphere of a room, making it sophisticated, soft, sensuous, welcoming, and luxurious.

Chairs and sofas may be transformed by slipcovers—from the soft warmth of velvet in winter to the cool pale greens and dusty roses of summer, and from the grandeur of damask to the simplicity of modern, functional white denim. However, you don't necessarily need to go to the trouble or expense of slipcovers. A length of fabric draped over a piece of furniture can change the whole mood of a room. Andrea Dern, for instance, uses her white crocheted bedcover to transform a tired sofa.

An old-fashioned formal dining-room table can become soft and romantic with a candle-lit crocheted lace cloth—or cool and welcoming for a summer lunch with a washed-out cotton floral print, evocative of the fresh smell of newly laundered, line-dried fabric, and of the ceremonies surrounding the hand-washing, wind-drying, sun-bleaching of household cotton and linen. Wash day, although hard work, was a ceremony of a kind, honoring both the quality of the cloth and the hand that made it.

An average, unexciting plastic patio chair becomes a thing of beauty by disguising the cushion with some lovely fabric.

Andrea covered this sofa in a Ralph Lauren sheet sewn inside out (inside out for more subtle color, a sheet for less cost than yardage).

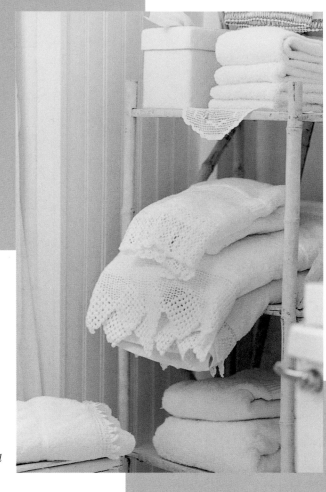

While on her husband's movie sets, Andrea lends her talents to crocheting lace borders, which she then applies to plain towels. (For those unable to crochet, pieces of lace and crochet are easily found and can be attached in this manner.)

Boxes and boxes of lace and crochet, waiting to be rummaged through, can be used in their original forms or can be applied to other items.

Draping a bedspread over a tired sofa is the simplest way to transform it, as Andrea did in her spare room.

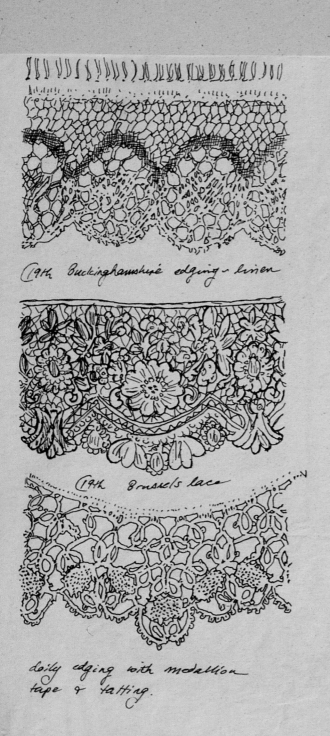

C19th Buckinghamshire edging ~ linen

C19th Brussels lace

doily edging with medallion tape & tatting.

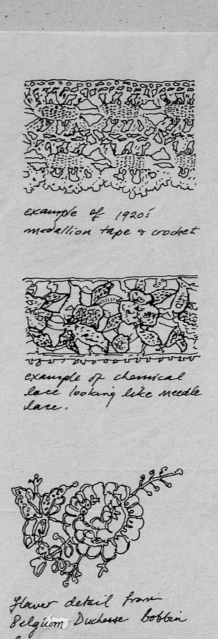

example of 1920's medallion tape & crochet

example of chemical lace looking like needle lace.

Flower detail from Belgium Duchesse bobbin lace.

Playful words brings a smile to my
face in memory of childhood.

chapter 3

COLLECTIONS
& ODDITIES

3

COLLECTIONS & ODDITIES
The Recognized Object

When you shop at a flea market you are on your own, without the reassurance that comes with the advertised, mass-produced purchase, accompanied by an illustration on the package showing you how to use it and where to put it. At the flea market, your own taste is your only guide—uninfluenced by what is currently being pushed in the shop windows and mail-order catalogues. Here you can express yourself in how you furnish your home, the clothes you wear, or the presents you give.

M. L. Peacor collects with a rhyme, reason, and method. Even common stones are gathered with an eye for their subtle tone and worn texture. Soothing to look at, calming to touch.

Objects that no longer work for their intended purpose can often be used for another. Allow yourself to be open to possibilities. If I see something I really like but don't know what to do with it, I pick it up, hold it, and after a while, I know or sense how I can use it. Some things take a little longer than others. I looked at a box of old, amber, slightly irregular glass chandelier drops for a long time before I saw a cache of paper weights and single-bar soap dishes…and many small original presents. Flea markets and antiques malls are full of objects that are either obsolete or damaged, unable to perform their original function. Many, like my chandelier drops, are tiny, while others are quite large. Andrea Dorn was charmed by a wheeled wicker marketing basket. Its wheels no longer roll easily, but she has painted it cream, lined it with an everyday trash bag, and keeps it in her kitchen, wheeling it around from one work surface to another to collect trash .

If you bake and decorate cakes, a pressed glass pedestal cake stand with a sterling silver base is a welcome find. But even if you don't know where your kitchen is located, don't pass by too quickly. Visualize it in the bathroom, perhaps displaying half a dozen cakes of soap in neutral tones. Or a large, plain white pottery bowl, perhaps originally intended for serving mashed potatoes to a family of eight, can be beautiful on a coffee table in a studio apartment, filled with smooth gray and green pebbles—tactile and pleasing to hold.

Although the wheels on this shopping trolley no longer stand up to street use, Andrea cleverly uses it in her kitchen to collect trash from different workspaces.

(previous spread)
It is easy to find cake plates similar to this one at flea market or antiques malls. This is perfect in my bathroom holding a few items I wanted separated from my array of toiletries.

*This common pearlized shell
provides a nest to store these soaps.*

A marble scalloped platter makes for a handsome display.

Karin Blake found this silver box. It has now become her traveling soap dish.

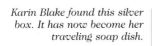

A lavender dish, although it may be too pretty to eat from, is a perfect complement for pink soap.

A plain white food dish!

I uncovered a box of decorative glass drops from an oversized chandelier. One can be a spot for soap, another a paperweight.
One for me and plenty more for gifts?

73

Sometimes an object that doesn't stand out on its own makes a better impression as one of a set, a concept rather than an accident. For example, a well-designed but far from delicate woven wire or metal basket—even one large and solid enough to have contained outdoor garbage—will fit in pleasantly indoors if it is one of several painted the same color. Maybe unexpectedly pink? Or lined with white linen or denim? Small antique bottles and kitchen jars are ideal for small flower arrangements and make thoughtful and inexpensive presents.

Although I view collecting as a suspect habit, developing a theme, particularly around a color, can be a highly effective decorating device. Sue Balmforth has shelves of yellow, green, and cream pottery—each piece pretty in itself, but the effect of the whole collection is greater than the sum of its parts.

Another exception to my antipathy toward collecting is Andrea Dern's use of small, individual pieces of crockery—restaurant or hotel creamers and butter plates—for entertaining. When she gives tea or dinner parties, each guest has his own tiny creamer and a plate just the right size for three pats of butter in front of his place setting.

I was charmed by these pink waste bins in the bathroom of a Beverly Hills club—a gentle reminder to me that I can always paint a common item in the most subtle way.

A wicker hamper can double as a side table and hide laundry as Andrea has done here.

While walking through flea markets and tag sales, I keep one eye open for aesthetically pleasing storage, ranging from Karin Blake's small silver box, used as a traveling soap dish, to a creaky, old-fashioned, wicker laundry basket in which large objects can be stored.

This is as good a moment as any to mention one of my basic beliefs pertaining to the functionally organized and visually pleasing home: Less is more. Storage should not be a way of keeping unsightly junk out of sight. I don't like the idea of my house being full of things I don't need, so what I do have deserves decent storage. It gives me a sense of calm order when I open a cupboard and find its contents in neat and logical order. I divide the things I store into three rough categories. If the item in my hand doesn't fit into one of them, I give serious thought to adding it to the recycling bin.

The first category is things you use every day—in the kitchen, bathroom, office, or closet. Be it an antique saucer for paper clips or a metal tin to hold socks, the storage container should be functional—an antique box, for instance—of the right size and pleasing to the eye. If architectural excellence or location is more important to you than square footage, you might consider the choices made by Nina and Lou and by M.L., who have made their storage containers attractive enough in color, proportion, and shape to contribute to their decor.

Nina and Lou—Nina is responsible for the lovely flower arrangements in my shop—live in a little house (450 square feet). Common sense and taste have gone a long way to solve this house's main problem, which is, of course, space. Much of the charm of this house comes from the ingenuity with which they have incorporated storage into the overall decor. Accessible and attractive storage (not stuffed and crammed) is easily accomplished with a collection of interesting containers, using them in ways other than originally intended. Their home is functional, hence balanced and beautiful.

A wire shopping basket, lined, holds some of Lou and Nina's linens.

This green metal tin can could hold a variety of items. Here it holds socks.

77

Work in progress at Andrea's—a watercolor sketch hangs below her hatboxes. The boxes provide storage space and are always useful for holding gifts instead of using giftwrap.

A sturdy hatbox becomes a foot rest under Nina's desk, as well as more storage.

The second category requires legitimate long-term or seasonal storage—larger, practically shaped containers for those tax returns and checkbook stubs you don't use but dare not throw away; a painted box for the Christmas tree ornaments; an antique trunk that doubles as a coffee table, where seasonal clothing may be packed away.

Finally, there is the "keep forever" box or drawer where you store the record and treasures of your life—love letters and milk teeth, your children's art and your grandfather's medals, a wedding invitation, postcards from camp. Nostalgia, souvenirs. These deserve a safe, special, and beautiful storage place—a hatbox, perhaps.

The perfect green metal trunk contains important paperwork behind Nina's desk.

Andrea and Bruce's bathroom has the feeling of a greenhouse. In this moist air her flowers thrive.
This green box is home to a mixture of her scent bottles.

The perfect container for the simple toilet roll.

M.L.'s son found one of these frogs in an expensive store—he begged his mom to buy it just to put stuff in it. She was then inspired to pick up another for pennies at a church sale.

Sue Balmforth will never pass up a wire basket. These are from the '20s, '30s, '40s, and '50s. Placed throughout the house, these evoke an interesting theme. They have a variety of uses— storage, waste, laundry.

Sue Balmforth builds collections as she finds these inexpensive pottery pieces. Grouping like colors makes a statement.

Andrea has gathered these creamers on her travels. When she has tea or dinner parties each guest has his or her own jug. Special!

M.L.'s pottery jar collection holds the various tools of her trade. The economical use of space in her home always leaves these items visible. Hence the attractive and practical display.

Petite butter dishes—one for each guest—at Andrea and Bruce's beach house. Only a couple inches in diameter, these tiny plates lend a lovely formality to an informal setting.

Since the stuff for sale at flea markets and antiques malls is usually one-of-a-kind secondhand or antiques, chances are you will not see your findings anywhere else. That is why it is so important to define your taste and develop your eye—to know what you like and to recognize it when you see it.

Less really is more.

Nina and Lou's pride in their house allowed for an old plaster molding found at a flea market to hang proudly over their door. It is their palace.

A simple request

TABLETOPS

Chapter 4

TABLETOPS

Informal Elegance and Graceful Nothingness

At M.L.'s house a found olive jar is to me an earthly elegance.

One of my favorite flea-market buys is a turn-of-the-century flowered porcelain bowl with a dull silver rim and base. The ceramic has, over the years, developed a slight crackle—not to be confused with "cracks." I never buy a bowl that is cracked, because it is unhygienic for food and impractical as a flower vase. I love the subdued tones, the tomato red of the design, and its low graceful shape. I use it for flowers—soft white floppy flowers with gray-green foliage give a pleasing "blowsy" effect. Even if the theoretical focal point of your living room is a sofa or mantelpiece, a vase of flowers carefully placed on a tabletop is sure to draw the eye. The same is true of the sparkle and twinkle of a cut-glass bowl. Such simple and unpretentious details add character and personality to a room.

Your table will most clearly reflect your taste if you place on it only what you actually need. Just be sure those objects are functional and beautiful. A table that holds an antique glass lamp, a bunch of flowers in a flea-market olive jar, and a book has no need for ornaments or frou-frou.

An old milk bottle stands with an unevenly painted vase. It's pretty enough with or without flowers as a tabletop display.

(on previous spread) Such a therapeutic task— warm sudsy water, ending with satisfaction of a job well completed.

I'm not quite sure how this porcelain and silver-trimmed bowl was originally used. I've found it's perfect for flowers, allowing them to wilt gently.

A jug decorated with lemons is lovely for these free-form roses.

*A vase with a life of its own.
The depth of texture and color
of this piece caught my eye as
I paced through the flea markets.
Tiny chips here and there were
camouflaged with nail polish.*

*M.L. put a lovely display of Gerber
daisies in this pot.*

*A table needs little more than a beautiful vase of flowers. This is a typical
example of a flea-market–found vase. I love Nina's flower arrangements.*

Nina and Lou's tiny kitchen is humble but beautifully practical. Dainty curtains replace cumbersome cupboard doors. A chopping block covers what was once an extra sink. The draining board is a safe resting place for an eclectic collection of old one-off dishes.

Sue adds delicacy by tying a fresh rose with twine to an unironed flea-market linen napkin. I love them.

(opposite page)
For weddings, birthdays, and all festive occasions there is not a prettier table than one arranged by Sue Balmforth. Here she mixes sturdy inexpensive restaurant seconds with English and French, delicate red, white, and pink glasses. The combination is perfect.

In the kitchen and the bathroom, I try to dispense with the extraneous and present and store what remains in as clean and simple a manner as I can. An antique porcelain dish on a white-tiled surface. An old glass scent bottle used as a bud vase.

The table at which you eat and about which family conversations take place can be greatly enhanced by what you bring back from the flea market. Whether you are feeding the children a spaghetti supper on hotel monogrammed white soup plates, pouring their milk into mismatched thirties milk-glass tumblers, and encouraging them to wipe their fingers on unironed and slightly worn cotton napkins; or setting the table for a festive Thanksgiving dinner, there is plenty of room for inexpensive creativity and imagination. The special occasions, weddings, birthdays, holidays, or dinner parties are occasions when family silver, heirloom wineglasses, or the pearl-handled fruit knives you inherited from your great-grandmother can be advantageously mingled with flea-market finds. This adds a sense of your own taste and imagination while ensuring enough serving dishes. Again, objects do not need to serve their original purposes. Sometimes extravagance and luxury is conveyed by using something grand for a more pedestrian purpose. Karin Blake uses blue and white flow-ware soup tureens—complete with lids and set on platters—as individual soup bowls, adding a touch of elegance and formality to the meal. Needless to say, the tureens do not need to match one another, although a similar or sympathetic color and approximately equal sizes helps.

A mixture of elegance, informality, and beauty—as in old silver, a worn napkin, and a fresh flower—can add grace to a dinner table and is infinitely preferable to the perfectly matched, pristine newness of settings sold by stores whose names are synonymous with luxury and high prices.

Milk glass is a sturdy, nicely detailed addition to any place setting.

(opposite page) Elegance needn't be lost with children's dinners of compulsory pasta. A chandelier from Bountiful sets the mood; the framed mirror was a keeper once I got it home from Santa Monica Flea Market. The purely decorative pastel painting reflects my palette perfectly. Sturdy milk glass and mismatched linens allow for heavy-handed sticky fingers.

These nothing metal jugs became something with flowers and the commitment to creating a collection.

Pressed glass is a very acceptable substitute for crystal and easy to find. Once again, the abundance is the statement.

(opposite page) Presenting each guest with their own individual pressed-glass bud vase at the dinner table is elegance on a budget. It can be your secret.

Even more than the dining-room table, the kitchen offers creative opportunities for using pretty and original flea-market treasure. The heavy earthenware jars that once held marmalade or peanut butter make pleasing containers for kitchen implements or may be used to store or even serve food. Old glass—bowls, glasses, cups, and saucers of pressed, plain, colored, or milk glass—is still easy to find at flea markets. It is so useful: as a substitute for fragile and expensive crystal; to display a bouquet of flowers; to store pens and pencils on the desktop or beside the telephone; or to hold toothbrushes and make-up brushes.

Every so often, I take everything off the tabletop, and give the ruffled, washed-out chintz a good shake. I feel as though I am not just getting rid of dust and wrinkles but bringing it back to life. When I put the objects back on the tabletop—the vase of fresh flowers, the newly dusted lamp, the small pile of books—the subtle alteration in their placement gives the objects a new life. This seems to prevent the "dead" feeling that pervades a room that, although perfectly clean, is not lived in. Because every object I move is one I have carefully chosen and thoughtfully placed, this activity is more a pleasure than a chore.

FLOW WARE

Flow ware is blue china: English, old, and gloriously imperfect. Before glazing was perfected, the blue patterns made by Staffordshire potters tended to bleed. Today these pieces, each slightly different, are both prized and collected—and a little harder to find.

KARIN BLAKE

"I am always rummaging through funny little shops," Karin Blake says. She is a decorator and collects primitive furniture and folk art. She comes from New England and now lives in Malibu. Her design sense is one of puritan elegance. Although her taste might seem to be aesthetically in conflict with Shabby Chic, it is surprising how often we admire the same look or are pleased by the same idea or object—her blue-and-white flow-ware mix-and-match dinner service, for instance. She has no inhibitions about combining flea-market and church-sale finds with more serious purchases from a crème-de-la-crème antiques shop. I like that.

She likes "the freedom of white." During her process of designing, she says, "I live in a space and wait. Some solutions are obvious, others emerge with time."

Karin Blake created this elegantly welcoming table. Over the years she has traveled from coast to coast, from churchyard sales to flea markets purchasing blue-and-white flow ware. She uses platters and terrines for individual plates and soup dishes, creating a sense of grandeur for each guest.

Mennecy-Villeroy Vase

Plymouth Covered Garniture Jar

Worcester Chocolate Pot With Domed Lid

Lowestoft Butter Boat

Wedgewood Ivy Pattern Plate

Wedgewood Ivy Pattern Bouillon Cup

Karin collects simple classic stoneware. So usefully functional, the quantity is the statement.

Peanut butter barrels: Karin has collected many; these two are in use in her kitchen.

This lovely cutlery was passed down to Karen from her grandmother—nicely complementing her collection of napkin holders, which holds her varied collection of linen.

Karin treats her linens with the respect age and delicacy deserve. They are laundered, laid on cardboard, tied with a ribbon, and plastic-wrapped. Karin can accept the original stains as the character of age.

Simple, simple, simple—a clear cut-glass lamp with a white linen shade quietly enhances any room.

Andrea picked up this smiling chap on her journeys. Cheerful whimsy. The shade's lining was so tattered that she simply removed it.

Andrea found this at Shabby Chic— another example of inspiration from her garden. A simple parchment shade is all this intricate lamp base needs.

A cool alabaster lamp—rewiring is all I had to do. In the realm of Shabby Chic this will complement any setting.

*Although a little harder to come by than in the past,
this Italian, delicately hand-painted chandelier is a
charming addition to Nina and Lou's house.*

Because I live at the beach, shells have become my natural decoration. My son loved this one, and I made it into a lamp by having an electrician wire it.

DRIFTING

Am I drifting? Am I focused?
Either answer is fine, just
so long as I'm aware.

DECORATIONS
chapter 5

DECORATIONS
The Thought That Counts

The celebration of an event is an acknowledgment of the importance of that event—wedding, christening, birthday, Thanksgiving, or Christmas—and the place it occupies in our lives. Celebration and ritual allow us to express our feelings of love, joy, and gratitude. The ceremony, the tradition, and the decorations and trappings are visible, tangible expressions of how we feel. They help us all to feel the same emotion at the same time. Afterward they become memories, and the decorations can become souvenirs, helping us to recall the emotions and the importance of an event.

(opposite page)
M.L. started her collection of mercury glass decorations with a couple of pieces from an expensive store. She later learned that by buying easily found old, brightly colored ornaments and gently washing and rubbing them in soapy water, she could transform them into pure silver mercury glass. As a final touch, she adds a plain gray ribbon. For Christmas M.L. hangs the smaller mercury balls on a topiary plant, which then becomes her Christmas tree.

I don't think these muted pastel Christmas ornaments could be any prettier.

(previous spread)
I found this multitiered papier-mâché wedding cake and didn't know what use I would find for it, but I knew I definitely had to have it. Since then it has been a dramatic yet welcoming entrance to two weddings. Both times I've draped it with fresh flowers, usually keeping the color monochromatic —cream on cream.

How we decorate is an expression of our individual style. Behind most decorating, for me, is thought, patience, imagination, and the satisfaction of making something that expresses love and affection. The wrapping of presents is a transitory form of decoration and allows me to give free rein to my creative imagination.

Some time ago I bought a very large papier-mâché three-tiered wedding cake and have used it to adorn the entrance to two weddings, decorating the cake with fresh flowers—in one pale color only—to make a festive combination of old and new. The wedding cake was a once-in-a-lifetime find, but there are some decorative items I come upon over and over again. The pale pink sleigh and creamy-toned reindeer—as special as I think it—is a common sight on my travels. Made of flaky wood, it is a warm and evocative respite from the garish colored neon and plastic decorations sold by the less distinguished of our chain stores.

Remnants of a shower. The workmanship is extraordinary.

(opposite page)
A creamy tissue bell with pink silk ribbons found in a box of like items. I was so attracted by the yummy color. An elegant subtle decoration for a shower or wedding.

These delicate velvet fruits were salvaged from the trim of a mirror.

These tiny beaded things I found at the Long Beach Flea Market.

Milliner's decorations I found at Lorraine Fogwell's store. They could be a gift in themselves, but I will use them as gift wrapping trim.

There would be little pleasure for me in spending a lot of money on mass-produced wrapping paper and ribbon to wrap and decorate the presents I give to those I love. I like the outward appearance of each gift to reflect some aspect of my taste, the taste of the person to whom I am giving the present, and possibly to contain a reference to the gift itself.

For me there is something a little sad about the gift-wrapped present sent directly from a department store or mail-order depot. I usually wrap a present in layers of pastel tissue or plain parcel paper or in an antique box. Then I decorate the parcel, either with old ribbon from the flea market or ribbons I tear from strips of plain muslin. I like to finish by adding some little one-of-a-kind decoration I have found on my travels: velvet strawberries from a discarded mirror; silver hat beading from a milliner's oddment box; silk or paper flowers; shells. I think the giving and receiving of a present should be a personal and pleasurable experience. The very effort and thought that goes into finding the decoration is reflected in the result and makes it beautiful.

Simple scallop shells are delicately decorated before they become decorations themselves.

Don't pass up limp or mashed up silk flowers and ribbons. Wave them over the spout of a boiling teakettle, and they will revive and pop back to life. (The steam will be very hot, so use tongs or a potholder.)

119

*Paper wedding flowers
with silk ribbon crying out
to be recycled—again.*

Flea markets and antiques malls offer a wealth of ribbon, shells, vintage silk, old boxes, and paper flowers. These can be used as you find them, or little knickknacks can be adapted for the decoration. If you look carefully you will find complete collections of decorations left over from parties or functions. Because these are often sold as job lots, by the boxful, you may find you have an additional jumble of assorted cards and decorations. Even if you end up throwing some of these away, you will still have made a good buy and saved money.

Silk and linen flowers often get passed by. Get into the habit of buying them. There is always use for them—as a gift, on a hat, or for decoration.

I store my spare decorations in a pretty little chest of drawers, similar to the one in which I keep my "keep forever" treasures. The little drawers keep the buttons, bows, flowers, shells, and ribbons separate. The miniature drawer knobs and the antique wallpaper finish remind me of the pleasures of original and creative decoration.

Whimsy off the beach and a leftover from something—somewhere.

*(opposite page)
Adding bits and bobs to packages wrapped in plain white parcel paper or in fabric remnants creates a wonderful vision and thought for a gift.*

120

Humility

HUMILITY is perpetual quietness of heart. It is to have no trouble. It is never to be fretted or vexed, irritable or sore, to wonder at nothing that is done to me, to feel nothing done against me. It is to be at rest when nobody praises me, and when I am blamed or despised; it is to have a blessed home in myself where I can go in and shut the door and kneel to my Father in secret and be at peace, as in a deep sea of calmness, when all around and about is trouble.

Words I aspire to.

chapter 6
APPAREL 6

APPAREL
Couture, Cashmere, and Camisoles

When I was a child, my sister Deborah, who always had artistic talents, collected antique clothes. She had a basket full of Victorian underskirts, Edwardian high-necked blouses, elegant tea-gowns, and glamorous evening dresses. On Sunday afternoons she would dress up in her finery. At the time I was not much interested, probably because she was my big sister. Later, as an adult designing costumes for commercials in England, I found that my appreciation of the old and the beautifully made grew; soon I was only interested in working on period productions. Choosing and designing contemporary clothes didn't interest me; I was most happy when researching period costumes and rummaging through baskets of old fabrics to find the right trim. I appreciated the romance of ruffles, draping, and extravagant touches. Although I no longer design costumes for commercials, it is a rare day that I do not wear something I bought at a flea market or, to an evening dress-up occasion, a vintage dress show.

PROM DRESSES
fancy dresses

(opposite page)
*Prom dresses found at the
Pickwick Vintage Textile Show:*
- *pale pink*
- *pale green*
- *muted pastels*
*—lovingly handsewn. Chances
are, as prom dresses, they only
have been worn once before
and are begging to be worn again.*

(previous spread)
*The translucent tulle of
these prom dresses evokes
an untouchable femininity.*

fancy dresses

The hang of this fabric, the draping of the train
and the delicacy of the detail (all hand done)
create a work of art in a dress. No fabric was
spared, and it wears beautifully.

circa
1930

129

original

tea stained

bleached

cold-water dyed.

This dress has such potential.
Hemline can be altered
Color can be changed.

Rose
pink

vintage
fashion
collection

My flea-market buys blend with the newer clothes in my wardrobe. I believe flea-market clothing should be worn unselfconsciously and not as a way of re-creating the past. I think of it instead as an opportunity to wear clothes of really lovely quality not available today or, if available, too expensive for everyday use.

It is the mixture of periods and styles that achieve the look I like and in which I feel most comfortable. I buy most of my jeans at flea markets and often wear them with a cashmere sweater. If I had spent five hundred dollars for new cashmere, it would spend most of its time between sheets of tissue paper in a drawer, but my ten- or fifteen-dollar cashmere cardigan gives me a luxurious feeling while I work, relax, or play with my children. Like nearly everything I buy at the flea market, my clothes are for living in—not for fancy dress, not for once-in-a-great-while occasions. My possessions are meant to be used, to be part of my and my children's lives, and to affirm a way of living that is free, comfortable, and aesthetically pleasing.

SWEATERS

Cashmere is an affordable luxury. Vintage-clothing stores and flea markets are places to look, but do check for moth holes. Jeanne, who works in my shop, has an enviable collection of cashmere pullovers and cardigans. I have been fooled many times by the gorgeous quality of sweaters she has bought for pennies.

Once vintage apparel was thought of as secondhand clothes, the very words evoking the image of smelly, torn hand-me-downs. If you were brave and lucky, you might find buttons or scraps of lace to use elsewhere. Today, vintage clothing may be found on the racks not only of flea markets and the Salvation Army but of fashionable main-street boutiques and even auction houses. Some of the specialized vintage-clothing shows or fancier shops offer "dead stock"—vintage clothing that has never been worn. These clothes, as you would expect, cost a little more. Another treasure of the elite vintage circles are European designer suits with the original label intact; the women who bought these expensive clothes in Paris or London often cut the labels out in order to smuggle them through U.S. customs.

This delicate camisole is a wonderful accent, for the innocent detail of hand workmanship. Someone cared enough to make this.

(opposite page) Often available in blue, white, black, and pink, these cardigans add interest to jeans and a tee-shirt or are elegant enough to finish off an evening outfit.

FLORAL PRINTS

A pink velvet bow nestled among a cluster of pink petals makes for such a fun and pretty hat.

The intricacy of these miniature gathers and pleats among the lavender rayon dress is a detail rarely found in the casual dresses of today.

The generous cut of this dress, combined with the faded floral print on fine voile, makes an innocent, simple, pretty summer frock.

Vintage apparel makes even more sense for those once-in-a-lifetime occasions than for day-to-day wear. A wedding gown or prom dress is the most expensive garment you will ever buy, if you calculate its cost against the number of times it is worn. We live in a time when our more formal and festive clothes are only worn occasionally. It's been a long time since anyone I know wore an evening dress until it became threadbare or frayed. The irony is that a vintage dress will be useful and attractive for years to come while this season's model, costing ten times as much, may seem a little dated by this time next year. The vintage gown may even become an heirloom. And I love the feel of vintage handmade clothes, the sense of once-extravagant couture or a simple day dress lovingly crafted by a mother for her daughter.

FLORAL

Detail of
sleeve with
smocking

*Although simplicity is the place to start, the qualities of this embroidery
and smocking contributes to the specialness of this top.*

PRINTS

The frivolous ruffles and the perfect fading of the print (from endless washing) makes this one of my most favorite and most worn flea-market finds.

The throwaway look of a summer slip dress from the '40s. The fine lawn fabric, the stunning print—little else is needed.

DRESSES

The choice and range of garments for sale at the flea market seems endless—quantities of rayon floral dresses, Victorian undershirts, silk nightdresses, my favorite pastel cashmere cardigans, and perfectly faded Levis. A pair of these Levis with a pale blue cashmere cardigan and a hand-embroidered white-on-white camisole, worn with a belt and shoes from one of today's designers, makes an elegantly casual, useful, and inexpensive outfit. On a warm summer day I like to wear a vintage floral nightie as a dress. Because it is a floral print (washed-out pinks and reds on an off-white background) and made of rayon, it looks and feels like a summer dress. However, if it looked like a nightie—a solid pastel, silky and lacy—no matter how pretty, I would not choose to wear it as a dress, out in public.

Rarely are affordable clothes cut on the bias today. This type of tailoring using the broadest expanse of fabric is more apt to be found in high-end designer lines. (Panels cut and pieced together are more economical). This is a 1940s floral print nightie, which was commonly cut on the bias, creating a sexy flattering silhouette. Found abundantly in silky solid pinks and creams, they remain lovely nightgowns. This being patterned, however, adapts beautifully as a day dress.

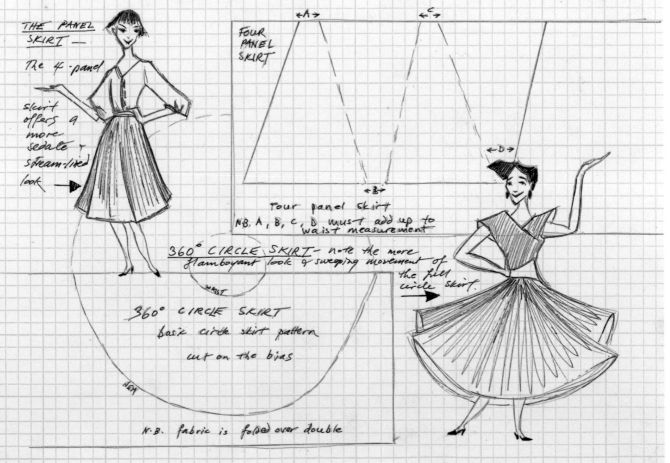

THE PANEL SKIRT —

The 4-panel skirt offers a more sedate + stream-lined look →

FOUR PANEL SKIRT

←A→   ←C→

←B→

Four panel skirt
N.B. A, B, C, D must add up to waist measurement

360° CIRCLE SKIRT - note the more flamboyant look & sweeping movement of the full circle skirt. →

WAIST

360° CIRCLE SKIRT
basic circle skirt pattern
cut on the bias

HEM

←D→

N.B. fabric is folded over double

GLOVES

gloves

Elbow-length, pink cotton gloves, with a tucked bow.

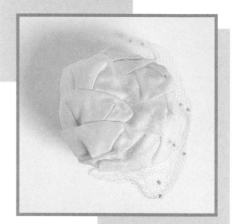

Short nylon, with loose ruffles.

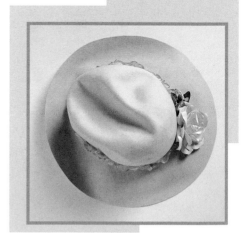

hats

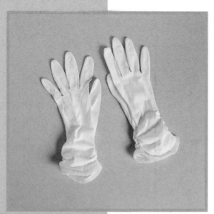

Fine gloves with pleats and gathers.

HATS

142

BAGS

In the past, hats and gloves had associations of formality —weddings and church on Sunday mornings—or privilege —suburban ladies' lunches, Ascot, and garden parties. The workmanship was very fine, and many of the gloves I find are handmade. I don't think of them as something for special occasions, but as an effective throwaway detail.

Handbags are inexpensive and are often made of supple leather, silk-lined, and designed and stitched with a standard of workmanship that would make their price prohibitive today. I often find a purse with an ornate clasp that seems almost royal, or sometimes I find a couture label. One of my favorite flea-market buys is a floral sewing bag with a light wooden handle. I carry it sometimes when I am wearing jeans and a white tee-shirt. It is one of the prettiest accessories I own, and people stop me in the street to admire it. These sewing bags are still easy to come by and not expensive. They were, however, meant to hold sewing—not bunches of keys and a Filofax—and should be treated with the care and respect their age and delicacy deserves.

Well-designed and once-expensive luggage often shows up at flea markets. It lasts forever and is worth considering for good-looking storage or other uses. Although it is often sophisticated and reminiscent of a time when the emphasis was on the voyage rather than the destination, it tends to be too large and heavy for the airline shuttle.

I discovered this ethnic, embroidered, secondhand sack in an old store in England. It comes on many flea-market trips now.

A vintage sewing bag gives me much pleasure and will one day be the inspiration for a new Shabby Chic fabric.

Classic, soft white leather drawstring purse. These bags are at the flea market by the dozen.

Secondhand clothing may come with imperfections, some of which can be overlooked and lived with. Others would be best served by a minor repair. In the case of jeans, I usually have them repaired by my local dry cleaner. They do quite an ornate patching job by overstitching. Most dry cleaners offer this service.

Due to my personal uniform of Levis, I relate to the fascination the Japanese have with jeans. They flock to American flea markets to buy old Levis by the truckload. If the size, the condition (button flies, not zippers), and the label is correct, a pair of Levis sold in the United States can fetch hundreds of dollars in Japan.

This fine lawn dress had a tiny tear in the back. Careful hand sewing disguised the flaw.

This blouse grew a hole after I bought it. In a hurry I crudely patched it, which I now find rather charming.

Although there are no real rules for buying vintage clothes, there are certain guidelines I follow. I carefully check the condition of anything I am considering. Faded elegance is appealing, but worn-out and tired garments are not.

That said, I don't write off any piece if it has a quality I particularly admire—a silk dress cut on the bias, for instance; a handmade white blouse; a well-tailored jacket. It is worth considering possible solutions, which are usually simple and inexpensive, to problems. Holes and tears can be darned or patched, hemlines may be shortened or, if there is enough fabric, lengthened. Lapels are easily cut down to a narrower style. Buttons can be replaced. I have more than once bought an imperfect bias-cut dress, chopped off the top, stitched it, and in a matter of minutes had a pretty new skirt.

Work you do not feel qualified or confident enough to undertake can be done by your local dry cleaner. In the case of complicated structural alterations, it may be wise to take it to a tailor.

Even the color is not hard to change. Never underestimate the ease and possibilities of tea-staining. White that is too stark or has grown dingy can be transformed into a softer, more flattering, old-fashioned sepia. Easy-to-use dyes and fading with sun or bleach can transform a pattern from the garish to the subtle and subdued.

Our clothes are an important reflection of who we are and how we see ourselves. At the flea market or a vintage-clothing show I am not limited to the colors and patterns, shapes, and lengths dictated by this season's fashions. Instead I have the pick of a hundred years of fashions and trends. I buy clothes and accessories of greater originality and a higher quality of workmanship and design than are offered in today's mass market. Because the selection of flea-market clothing is not driven by season or fashion, I can choose what I want, when I want it, saving not only money but time. Flea markets and vintage-clothing shops give me a varied and reasonably priced way of owning and wearing something beautiful and unique.

PATCHES

Whatever became of the conversations
that took place after the
"you wash and I'll dry," decision was reached?

chapter 7
FINISHED
HOMES

FINISHED HOMES
The Full Circle

My home is never quite "finished." It is a living thing and as such develops and changes. My furniture and fabrics become older and worn; they settle in and evolve. New life is introduced by the changes I make, some as permanent as painting a room, some as temporary as buying a bunch of flowers. My house is lived in, for living in. One of the places I find new life is at flea markets.

It may take me a few trips to find what I am looking for. And even when I do, more time may be required to restore it. Instant gratification is not an expectation here, nor would I wish it to be. To get something right, and for it to truly reflect my personality and taste, takes time.

This chapter will look at several homes that are "finished" to the extent that they are comfortably lived in by people of taste and discrimination, "unfinished" in the sense that they are living, changing places.

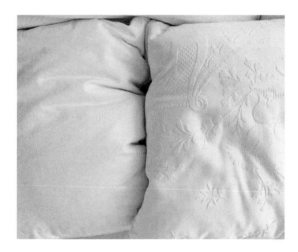

A touch of class is added to a huge, slipcovered Shabby Chic sofa by mixing pieces of a vintage bedcover with basic white denim. I am able to use slightly damaged—and more economical—bedcovers here, because I can cut around any flaws. The sofa wraps around a flea-market coffee table. Once upon a time it was a clunky oak table. I added some simple beaded molding (available at a good hardware store) to give it just a little glamour and then painted it cream. All contribute to a cozy space for Jake.

A fine lawn bedcover doubles as a curtain. In my office at home, I need only to diffuse the light.

(opposite page)
This is one of my most creative spots in the whole world. A dear friend of mine painted this happy picture for me. The desk was a Carpenteria find, and what was once a patio table I transformed into a seat by adding a cushion.

MY HOME

My house is lived in, for living in, and for life. Balance is one aspect of this philosophy: a balance of function, beauty, and comfort. My living room contains flowers and a piano for life, good lighting for function, and beautiful, enveloping seating for comfort. The flea-market coffee table was originally a dark clunky oak—I added beading and molding and painted it a calming cream. Instead of heavy and cumbersome, it is now lighter, delicate—in harmony with the room. I made an antique bedcover into large, comfortable, and decorative cushions, which add a touch of class and a cozy invitation to the white denim slipcovers on my Shabby Chic sofa. My office has gradually accumulated a series of objects that are just "off." Each on its own would not quite make it, but in combination they make my surroundings an inspiring and stimulating place to work. Beauty and balance bring peace. So does an acceptance of the impermanence of both living and inanimate objects. The flowers die and are replaced with others equally beautiful but different. A piece of the china we use for dinner breaks. We are sorry to lose it, but because we eat off plates in a harmony of colors and shapes rather than a pattern that matches exactly, the piece will be replaced. The set of china will continue, slightly different, perhaps slightly richer. This reusing of the old, the worn, and the shabby allows objects to meet their natural fate.

An abundance of certain items in the bathroom represents luxury to me, such as white towels and an array of soaps. Here wouldn't be the usual spot for watercolors—but why not? Every area deserves decor. This practical mirror was a flea-market find—the shelf detail makes it for me.

This small pink desk from Summerland Antiques passed my inspection, allowing its somewhat cumbersome wooden knobs to remain. The white wicker bench has an oversized pillow plopped on it.

This tall, slender chest of drawers makes a lovely pedestal for this doll house.

Gathers tacked in place with a tiny bow create a ruffle of perfection. A lampshade poised on a hand-painted glass lamp base is a cozy accessory.

155

This was one of those odd items
that caught my eye, because I knew
that one day I would find a use for
it. Now it is a dumping ground for
my daughter's hair accessories.

The brightly colored fine cloth became my daughter's bed cover.

A hand-painted trash can—quite a common find
—is a nice excuse for more flowers.

This pink shelf was hung without further ado.
It was the pink that caught my eye.

Sue Balmforth had a local upholsterer restore the original frame of her sofa. She added "tons" of down to bring her cushions back to plump life; she then slipcovered the whole piece in lovely floppy yellow linen. The ottoman, covered loosely in a nineteenth-century toile fabric, is forced to do double duty when a 1940s silver tray is placed on it. (It was found dull at the flea market and polished until it shone).

SUE BALMFORTH AND BOUNTIFUL

The home in which change is most constant and most evident belongs to Sue Balmforth. Sue is a designer who lives on the premises of Bountiful, her antiques shop. The large-scale architectural elements, statuary, and columns make the atmosphere of Bountiful dramatic and theatrical. Sue is dedicated to her work and has a fabulous eye; she keeps an enormous stock so there is a luxurious feeling of plenty—more beautiful French and Italian chandeliers twinkling overhead than you could imagine; lovely, flaky, painted Early American country armoires; European dressers and vanities hand painted in pale colors with floral details and carved rose moldings; quantities of fine wicker chairs hanging from the ceiling. Bountiful is arranged so that there is an opulent sense of layering—vignettes leading to further vignettes, the mercury glass story leading to the crystal story in turn leading to the looking-glass story—and one can see the range of beautiful objects, giving a generous depth of comparison. Sue understood the potential uses of architectural salvage very early on, transforming it into coffee tables, large mirrors, candlesticks, and picture frames.

This is Beatrice, Sue's favorite creature in the whole world.

Sue's scrumptious bedroom can vary from week to week and shipment to shipment. Today it contains a delicate nineteenth-century French antique bedroom suite and is lit by a gorgeous handmade French chandelier, yet can still accept a humble breakfast tray. This 1920s handpainted American tray would have been given as a wedding gift years ago. A thought! Penni Oliver, a friend and associate of Sue at Bountiful, has created a line of lamp shades. She collects pieces of vintage textile and lace, which she then painstakingly hand-sews into delicate one-of-a-kind shades.

159

A vignette at Bountiful. Once again showing Sue's acceptance of mixing whimsy with the serious. Chipped bowling pins and painted trays from the flea market stand proudly under the twinkle of a posh chandelier.

One of Sue's genius creations is the use of salvaged tin ceilings to frame old paintings found on her travels. A quiet collection of lavender bottles dispels any sense of intimidation. A humble iron outdoor table is as significant as the company it keeps.

Her restoration of damaged pieces is very loyal to the original—broken chandelier drops are replaced with antique crystal; furniture is mended with hardware and hinges from the correct period. Because the objects in her home are part of her stock, they are constantly sold and replaced. The transient nature of her surroundings and possessions might cause anxiety and disorientation in a less adaptable person, but because Sue is original and ingenious, it merely gives scope to her imaginative creativity.

I particularly admire and enjoy Sue's confident mixture of flea-market finds with her up-market antiques. She says, "The accessories are absolutely key to creating a look when you decorate." Everything in Bountiful is for sale—including her bed and the elegant vintage linen that dresses it.

At the edge of Sue Balmforth's bedroom today sits a beautiful, friendly, pale green chair ready to be plopped into place. To me it's like Cinderella waiting to go to the ball. The chair is a 1920s American reproduction of a French chair, so it will easily fit in with her upscale French furniture.

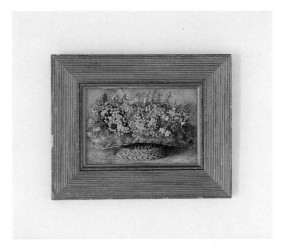

M.L. rescued this decorative floral print from the trash.

M. L. PEACOR

M. L. Peacor is also a designer. Perhaps her greatest design achievement is her own home. She chose her house—a 1930s cottage—for architectural excellence and location rather than size (650 square feet), and her use of space could be a lesson to us all. There is in the entire house no wasted or hidden space; M.L. has made a virtue of storage, and because all containers are in plain view, they clearly reflect her palette—creamy shades of white, yellow, blue, and green. The pale blue drugstore folders for her files, the glazed jars that hold her pencils—all blend with the bare books on her shelves. M.L. dislikes the bright and discordant contrasts of dust jackets and prefers the muted greens, grays, and blues of the books themselves.

In order to accommodate herself and her two sons in an essentially small but aesthetically pleasing space, M.L. has cleverly made most key items of furniture serve more than one function. At night her living room becomes her bedroom: her cushy yellow linen Shabby Chic sleeper sofa becomes her bed, with pastel poplin sheets, down pillows, and a duvet; the pale green painted picnic bench from the dining room becomes her bedside table. Because everything has its place, M.L. can quickly and easily make the space change from one function to another in a way that never compromises.

There are no hidden corners in M.L.'s functional home. Her Shabby Chic sleeper sofa is opened every night as her living room transforms into her bedroom. A pale green painted picnic bench borrowed from the dining room converts into her bedside table at night. In the distance the same pale green paint is used on a basket that holds bills and sits atop a creamy yellow desk. With everything visible, M.L. takes great care to sustain her palette, down to the littlest detail.

M.L. collects books of interest to her but dislikes dust jackets. Their removal often reveals M.L.'s restrained color palette of greens, gray-greens, and blues.

The house is equally cheerful and visually pleasing at all hours of the day or night. She has a great natural sense of color and an original and creative mind but modestly recounts how sometimes her memory inspires her eye: "I just need to see something in an expensive store once and then I know to look out for these things in other places." She describes how she bought a "frog" (the wire bases that stabilize flower arrangements in vases) for her son in an expensive shop—he saw it and really wanted it for "putting little things in"—some time later she saw a similar frog at a rummage sale and picked it up for a dollar. Sometimes we have to see an object in a grander context to recognize its real value.

M.L. got these wonderful, dusty, green, old-fashioned folders from a drugstore. She files and categorizes tear sheets from magazines, which she later refers to when on a design job. She applied flea-market-found jam jar labels for easy identification.

This work table doubles as everything does in M.L.'s compact home. It was originally from Scotland; she painted it pale green and then cleverly added an old wooden tape measure to the side to make measuring fabric easy.

Andrea found this frame dark and containing a portrait from the 1800s. Her beautiful rendering of lilacs now takes its place.

ANDREA AND BRUCE DERN

Andrea Dern is an artist, whose floral oil paintings I love. She and her husband, actor Bruce Dern, live in a house overlooking the ocean in Malibu.

Although the Dern house is quite large—an ever-expanding cottage, enchanted, rambling, full of little staircases and extraordinary light—every room feels as though it is lived in. The Derns have been there for twenty-five years, and Andrea, with a combination of time, life, taste, flowers, and lots of white paint, has produced a home—accented with wicker, flowers, and floral prints—that offers a warm and pleasant atmosphere. The house feels full and at the same time uncluttered. Each object has both its use and its place, and is the result of the imaginative and intelligent blend of materials at hand as well as an artist's taste.

Andrea's studio and her garden overlap. Her flower paintings bring the garden into the studio, and her paintings ensure her house is full of flowers even during the months when her garden is dormant. The briefest visit to Andrea's studio is enough to reveal that she loves what she does, and the environment is one of pleasure in creation, of life enhanced by the smell of the paint mingled with the scent of the flowers. Her artist's eye has designed a garden that is free-form, loose, and inextricably linked to her art. Andrea knows a good deal about her plants and flowers. Not only does she paint them and arrange them in vases around her house but she plants them and takes care of her garden herself.

Andrea and Bruce moved into this wonderful beach cottage twenty-five years ago. Very little in their home has escaped whitewash. The floors and the hutch were all transformed with white paint treatments in varying degrees.

This is Andrea's favorite cup in the world.

(opposite page)
Andrea found this somewhat irregular frame at Bountiful and loved it so much that she painted a picture to fit. The roses are Madam Alfred Carriere (rose paintings available at Shabby Chic).

The Violet Room—this room contains Andrea's gardening books among a theme of violet (her mother's name). The desk came with the house. She painted it white and added a mirror on top for extra reflective light.

Andrea's painting brushes.
Andrea's painting palette.

(previous spread)
Andrea's art studio has a natural evolution. Although this space wasn't designed, pieces of furniture were added as needed. Consequently it has a strong sense of function and necessity.

Andrea painted large checks atop this common rush mat, which created a unique effect and made the mat less susceptible to spills and crumbs in the seams. Brilliant!

Andrea applied her talents to this simple round mat, too.

This white vanity from Shabby Chic sits quietly in reflection.

Andrea's style is clever but not contrived; she creates a theme and avoids perfection. There is reasoning to her ways.

175

This is Andrea and Bruce's other living space. A tall dark dining table became a short white coffee table. Even the standing lamp that was once brass got the white treatment.

Nestled in Andrea's friendly garden, I found baskets in the colors of my palette.

Andrea and Bruce's Badger naps in a bundle of laundry placed in a lovely basket and stand from Bountiful.

A mirror found by Andrea at Shabby Chic was fit for royalty, but had been toned down with a whitewash.

Andrea's garden—her inspiration for her art— her roses, allowed to grow informally, create an air of tolerance.

When Andrea's garden needs a gentle watering, these do the job. The moral of this story is, "Don't walk away from something if the color is wrong."

A mercury glass ball, placed casually on a stick in Andrea and Bruce's garden. A gem.

Tucked away among the flowers, this happy girl poses. Little chips here and there are acceptable, as with all of us.

179

The shell mirror was the first purchase Andrea made when she and Bruce moved into their home. Inexpensive, it creates an eclectic corner in which to reflect.

This small dining room of Andrea and Bruce's was cleverly expanded with the simple use of mirrors (beveled, of course). Once again tables and chairs are white. Andrea wonders whether it's time to give the table a new coat —I advise her not to, because I believe it's at the perfect stage of chic now.

A collection of Depression glass sparkles, as fine as any crystal.

Barry and Lili Gross uncovered this stunning stenciling that frames their entranceway while they were renovating their house. Such detail deserves to be complemented. A French chandelier welcomes their guests. The friendly, unassuming hand-hooked rug balances the informal elegance. A flea-market dresser is adorned with a selection of shells and dried flower displays.

BARRY AND LILI GROSS

Barry and Lili Gross live in a 1940s Spanish-style house on the beach that exudes hospitality, comfort, and warmth. These qualities—and a mixture of tradition and elegant bohemianism—become evident as soon as one comes through the door. The stenciling around the entranceway was uncovered when they renovated the house—a pleasant surprise under layers of wallpaper—and the cement is chipped and flaked so the pattern is mottled and irregular. Usually I find stenciling a little too perfect, but here the uneven surface causes it to take on some of the qualities of a trompe l'oeil. The Grosses celebrated this find by dressing up the space with a French chandelier—mostly crystal but with a sprinkling of purple drops—and, for balance and contrast, a welcoming and humble hooked rug.

The house's essential feeling is one of family and fiesta. There is constant relaxed entertaining and someone always seems to be napping. The design and decor of the beach house is geared toward the comfort and feeding—with delicacies always arranged in an appetizing and original way—of a large number of family and friends. In the living room a large stack of futons is covered by an even larger white denim sack—an original, almost eccentric choice in an otherwise traditional room. Covered with cushions, like every other comfortable surface in the house or on the deck, it invites you to plop down wherever you are. The practical white denim can be unzipped and laundered when there is a build-up of sea salt or if a guest spills a glass of wine.

*(opposite page)
Barry and Lili's
princess. Her room
is decorated with
flea-market finds and
vintage textiles. Susie
Cohen (Lili's sister),
a designer, combined
scraps of vintage lace,
damask, and floral
broadcloth to create a
dreamlike window
treatment for her niece's
bedroom. The velvet
throne is paired with a
modest needlepoint
footstool. The headboard
and bedside table
are fun, inexpensive,
found treasures,
able to withstand
inevitable sticky hands
and doodles.*

*On Barry and Lili's shaded deck sits a royal blue tiled table, which got the white treatment for
its legs, giving it a French Provincial feel. Their plastic patio furniture is made stylish by covering the seat cushions with unexpectedly classy fabric and then layering them with old pieces of
beaded cloth.*

A carefully and hospitably planned deck has a balance of sun and shade; the furniture is practical and comfortable—huge futons in spring floral colors, covers made by a local seamstress, and extravagantly fine fabric on the cushions lend a touch of grandeur to the functional plastic outdoor furniture. There is a cheerful jumble of color, and the essential ordinariness of basic outdoor furniture is transformed by Barry and Lili's concentration on pleasure and function. There is an inviting hammock, and quantities of beach towels are stacked in a large wooden poled box.

Five houses. The sizes and functions vary from an elegant antiques shop, whose owner lives on the premises, to an informal beach house full of guests, children, and dogs to a family who insist on gracious living in the smallest possible space. Yet each home has several things in common. None has been "done" by an outside decorator; none shows evidence of money unnecessarily spent nor of conspicuous consumption; each has included worn relics of the past, bought at flea markets, in either their original form or imaginatively adapted for another use. In all these homes the passing of time has seasoned the look and atmosphere. These homes have evolved not by being left to their own devices but by a watchful, practical, and imaginative eye constantly ensuring that they adapt and grow to serve their function and please the eye while doing so. Balance. Beauty. Comfort.

Barry and Lili's luxurious deck is inexpensively decorated but lacks nothing in comfort and pleasure to the eye. Basic futons are hidden with easily removable floral chintz covers (made by a local seamstress). Mix-and-match collections of throw pillows are tossed around casually. Bath mats act as rugs. A wooden poled box is home to an assortment of towels.

Friendly birds sit on Andrea's table.

BLESS THIS HOUSE

BLESS this house, O Lord we pray,
   Make it safe by night and day;
Bless these walls, so firm and stout,
   Keeping want and trouble out;
Bless the roof and chimney tall;
   Let Thy peace lie over all;
Bless this door, that it may be
   Ever wide to welcome Thee.

a prayer for my home.

Sav-on

70% Isopropyl
Rubbing
Alcohol

WARNING: FLAMMABLE. KEEP
AWAY FROM FIRE OR FLAME.

Rubefacient

16 FL OZ (1 PT) 473 mL

WD-40

• Stops Squeaks
• Protects Metal
• Loosens Rusted Parts
• Frees Sticky Mechanisms

FLAMMABLE CONTENTS
UNDER PRESSURE
CONTAINS PETROLEUM DISTILLATES
KEEP OUT OF REACH OF CHILDREN
READ CAUTIONS ON BACK

Rit
LIQUID DYE

UNSCENTED EXTRA SUPER HOLD

AQUA
NET

Professional
y Hair Spra

The
Original

Woolite
FINE FABRIC WASH

CARE YOU CAN TRUST
No Shrinking, Stretching, Fading

354925

16 FL OZ (1 PT

BROWN

RESOURCES

chapter 8

FABRIC CARE

Washing

'WOOLITE' IS RECOMMENDED FOR WASHING ANY DELICATE FABRICS, VINTAGE CLOTHING, LINGERIE, SILKS, AND WOOL BLANKETS. USE COLD WATER, SOAK AND RINSE WELL. AIR DRY. OLD WOOLEN BLANKETS MAY BE MACHINE WASHED WITH WOOLITE TO SOFTEN THEM. AIR DRY, PREFERABLY OUTSIDE.

WASHING LACE: ANYTHING WITH LACE EDGING SHOULD BE HAND·WASHED. LAY FLAT TO DRY AND WHILE STILL DAMP, PAT INTO SHAPE WITH YOUR FINGERS. IT IS A GOOD IDEA TO WAIT FOR LACE TO DRY COMPLETELY BEFORE ATTEMPTING TO IRON IT.

CLEANING VINTAGE LINENS: WASH IN WARM WATER WITH A MILD DETERGENT AND A NON-CHLORINE BLEACH LIKE 'CLOROX 2' ON THE GENTLE CYCLE. FOLLOW BLEACHING DIRECTIONS ON THE PACKAGE. DELICATE PIECES SHOULD BE WASHED BY HAND. FOR STUBBORN STAINS, TRY A CHLORINE BLEACH SUCH AS REGULAR 'CLOROX' OR 'SNOWY BLEACH', BUT BEAR IN MIND, SOME OLDER OR FRAGILE PIECES MAY NOT STAND THE STRAIN OF BLEACHING OR EVEN MACHINE WASHING. FOR A NATURAL BLEACHING AGENT TRY RUBBING A STAIN WITH A LEMON CUT IN HALF. *

Bleaching

NEVER POUR BLEACH DIRECTLY ONTO FABRIC. ALWAYS DILUTE BLEACH BEFORE ADDING FABRICS TO THE WATER. IT IS A GOOD IDEA TO TEST THE FABRIC FIRST BEFORE BLEACHING THE ENTIRE PIECE. SOME FABRICS MAY YELLOW FROM BLEACHING AND SOME OLDER FABRICS MAY FALL APART. THERE IS ALWAYS A BIT OF RISK WITH THIS METHOD.

THE 'CLOROX' CO. DOES NOT RECOMMEND USING BLEACH FOR FADING AS IT CAN RESULT IN AN UNEVEN LOOK AKIN TO TIE-DYE. TO REMOVE COLOR THEY RECOMMEND 'RIT' OR 'TINTEX' COLOR REMOVER. FOR QUESTIONS ABOUT USING BLEACH, YOU CAN CALL THE 'CLOROX' CO. AT: (800) 292 2808 FROM 9 AM → 5.30 PM E.S.T.

Tea Staining

(NOTE: THE FOLLOWING TECHNIQUE RESULTS IN AN ATTRACTIVE, BUT NOT PERMANENT EFFECT.)

TO AGE FABRICS WITH A GENTLE OVERALL CREAM COLOR, SOAK IN A BATH OF TEA WATER. MAKE A TEABAG SOLUTION WITH WARM WATER. AFTER SOAKING THE ARTICLE RINSE WELL IN COLD WATER. THE NUMBER OF TEABAGS TO AMOUNT OF WATER AND LENGTH OF SOAK TIME DEPENDS ON QUANTITY OF FABRIC, HOW FAST A PARTICULAR FABRIC TAKES THE COLOR AND THE DARKNESS DESIRED. (THE COLOR WILL BE LIGHTER WHEN DRY, AND NATURAL FABRICS TAKE COLOR MORE READILY THAN SYNTHETIC ONES.) THIS IS A TECHNIQUE THAT REQUIRES YOU TO EXPERIMENT!

Dying

'RIT' DYE IS EASY TO COME BY AND IS EVEN SOLD AT MANY SUPERMARKETS. IT COMES IN A POWDERED OR LIQUID FORM. THE LIQUID IS EASIER TO USE TO OBTAIN AN EVEN RESULT. FOR DYING FABRICS, FOLLOW DIRECTIONS ON PACKAGE.

Color Removal

Rit COLOR REMOVER

TO FADE OUT FABRICS WHICH MAY BE TOO BRIGHTLY COLORED USE A COLOR REMOVER PRODUCT SUCH AS ONES MANUFACTURED BY 'RIT' OR 'TINTEX'.

*
AN OLD TIME WAY OF REMOVING STAINS FROM TABLE LINENS IS TO LAY THEM OUTSIDE ON THE GRASS BEFORE SUNDOWN AND LET THE DEW SOAK IN OVERNIGHT. IT IS SAID THE DEW WILL DRAW OUT THE STAINS AND THE SUN WILL FINISH BLEACHING THEM CLEAN THE NEXT DAY.

N.B. WHEN WORKING WITH THE ABOVE METHODS (E.G. DYING, STAINING, BLEACHING ETC.) IT IS ADVISABLE TO WEAR RUBBER GLOVES.

TIPS FOR TRANSFORMING TREASURES

USE ALCOHOL TO REMOVE GLUE RESIDUE FROM GLOSSY PORCELAIN. GLUE SHOULD BE GENTLY ABRADED WITH AN EMERY BOARD FIRST, AND THEN WIPED WITH A SOFT CLOTH DIPPED IN RUBBING ALCOHOL. TO CLEAN THE CRYSTALS ON CHANDELIERS, WIPE WITH A CLOTH MOISTENED WITH ALCOHOL.

A SINK FULL OF WARM WATER, NOT HOT, MIXED WITH 1/4 CUP OF CLEAR AMMONIA IS EXCELLENT FOR CLEANING GLASS. SOAK FOR A FEW MINUTES, THEN RINSE AND DRY GENTLY. NEVER PUT OLD GLASS PIECES IN THE DISHWASHER. SEE: MISCELLANEOUS SIDEBAR.

SOME SMALL PAINTBRUSHES ARE USEFUL FOR GENTLE CLEANING OF INTRICATE PORCELAIN FIGURES, VASES, LAMPS AND SUCH. YOU CAN EASILY DUST AND REMOVE GRIME FROM CREVICES AND DECORATIVE MOLDINGS WITH A CLEAN, SOFT BRISTLE BRUSH. KEEP SOME ON HAND FOR SMALL PAINT REPAIR JOBS ON VASES OR LAMPS.

CLEAN STAINED ENAMELWARE BY SOAKING FOR AN HOUR OR TWO IN A BATH OF ONE TABLESPOON OF BAKING SODA ADDED TO A SINKFUL OF HOT SOAPY WATER. TO REMOVE PENCIL, INK OR CRAYON MARKS FROM WALLS OR PAINTED SURFACES, RUB WITH A DAMP CLOTH DIPPED IN DRY BAKING SODA. THIS CAN BE USED TO RUB OFF COFFEE OR TEA STAINS ON CHINA CUPS.

TO CLEAN POLISHED MARBLE, USE WHITE CHALK MOISTENED WITH A LITTLE BIT OF WATER AND RUB GENTLY.

USE TO BRIGHTEN WHITE LINENS AND VINTAGE FABRICS. SEE: FABRIC CARE SECTION

REINFORCE JOINTS ON WOODEN CHAIRS AND TABLES, AND MAKE SMALL REPAIRS TO PICTURE FRAMES OR SHELVES WITH THIS GLUE. FOR A GOOD BOND, APPLY TO BOTH SIDES AND SECURE WHILE DRYING WITH SOME SORT OF CLAMPING DEVICE OR STRING UNTIL THE FOLLOWING DAY.

GESSO CAN EASILY BE USED FOR A WHITE-WASH FINISH ON WOODEN FURNITURE. USED BY ARTISTS FOR PREPARING CANVAS, IT CAN BE FOUND IN ART SUPPLY STORES.

HAIRSPRAY CAN BE USED TO REMOVE MARKING PEN, TAPE AND PRICE STICKER RESIDUE FROM GLASS. SPRAY ON AND WIPE OFF THOROUGHLY. SPRAY HAIRSPRAY ON ROSES TO PRESERVE THEM AND HANG THE FLOWERS UPSIDE DOWN UNTIL THEY HAVE DRIED COMPLETELY, AT LEAST ONE WEEK.

A LEMON, CUT IN HALF AND DIPPED IN SALT, CAN BE USED TO REMOVE TARNISH FROM OLD COPPER ITEMS. LEMON CAN BE RUBBED ONTO FABRIC STAINS SUCH AS INK, JUICE, OR RUST AS A NATURAL STAIN REMOVER.

AIRPLANE MODEL PAINT CAN BE PURCHASED AT ANY HOBBY STORE AND MANY TOY STORES. IT IS GOOD TO KEEP A SUPPLY OF COLORS ON HAND TO MAKE TOUCH-UP REPAIRS ON LAMPS, CERAMIC, PORCELAIN, FURNITURE, ETC.

A GREAT TOUCH-UP PRODUCT FOR CHIPS ON VASES AND OTHER PAINTED SURFACES. IT IS WATERPROOF WHEN DRY, AND COMES IN A MYRIAD OF PASTELS AND BRIGHTS SO YOU CAN EASILY MATCH COLORS.

THIS IS A VERY EASY WAY TO REMOVE OLD TAPE AND PRICE TAG RESIDUE. JUST RUB A VERY SMALL AMOUNT OF PEANUT BUTTER ON THE STICKY TAG WITH YOUR FINGER AND WIPE OR WASH OFF. WORKS WELL ON GLASS, COPPER AND BRASS.

'RIT' DYE IS SOLD IN POWDERED OR LIQUID FORM IN ABOUT 50 COLORS. IT IS EASIER TO OBTAIN AN EVEN HUE WITH THE LIQUID AS YOU DON'T HAVE TO WORRY ABOUT THE DYE CRYSTALS DISSOLVING COMPLETELY. SEE: FABRIC CARE SECTION. IT CAN ALSO BE USED TO STAIN UNFINISHED WOOD FURNITURE, FRAMES OR SMALL SHELVES IN A VARIETY OF SHADES. SEE: MISCELLANEOUS SIDEBAR.

KEEP SOME SANDPAPER ON HAND FOR QUICK REPAIRS TO ROUGH EDGES. THE FINEST SAND-PAPERS GIVE THE GENTLEST EFFECT. EVEN EMERY BOARDS ARE HANDY FOR GETTING INTO SMALL PLACES.

YOU CAN USE A BLACK OR BROWN SHOE POLISH TO DARKEN OVER-BRIGHT METAL HINGES ON CABINETS. APPLY SPARINGLY WITH A SOFT CLOTH AND RUB INTO GROOVES. THIS IS NOT PERMANENT AND ALSO SHOULD NOT BE USED NEAR FABRIC OR ON PLACES WHERE PEOPLE WILL TOUCH, SUCH AS DRAWER PULLS OR KNOBS.

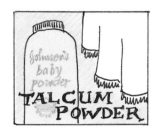

TALCUM POWDER IS A GOOD AID IN STAIN REMOVAL. REMOVE AS MUCH OF THE STAIN AS POSSIBLE BY BLOTTING WITH A CLEAN CLOTH. APPLY TALCUM POWDER AND LET IT SIT UNTIL THE POWDER BECOMES DISCOLORED BY ABSORBING THE STAIN; ABOUT 10 MINUTES. WIPE OFF WITH A CLEAN CLOTH. REPEAT IF NECESSARY.

IMMERSING FABRICS IN A BATH OF TEABAGS AND WARM WATER WILL IMPART A DELICATE AGED TONE TO THE CLOTH. SEE: FABRIC CARE SECTION.

VERY FINE GRADE STEEL WOOL DIPPED IN REGULAR VEGETABLE OIL CAN BE USED TO GENTLY RUB OFF THE RUST ADHERING TO OLD CUTLERY AND METAL HARDWARE.

WASH OLD BLANKETS IN 'WOOLITE' TO SOFTEN THEM. SEE: FABRIC CARE SECTION.

INDEX OF INTERIOR DESIGNERS

AND DESIGN SERVICES REFERRED TO IN THIS BOOK

Sue Balmforth
Bountiful
1335 Abbot Kinney Road
Venice, CA 90291
(310) 450-3620

Karin Blake
Karin Blake Interiors
49 A Malibu Colony
Malibu, CA 90265
(310) 456-8010

Susan Cohen
Susan Cohen Interiors
2118 Wilshire Boulevard, Suite 962
Santa Monica, CA 90403
(310) 828-4445

M. L. Peacor
M. L. Peacor Interior Design
1126 Idaho Avenue
Santa Monica, CA 90403
(310) 451-7787

Shabby Chic – Los Angeles
1013 Montana Avenue
Santa Monica, CA 90403
(310) 394-1975

Shabby Chic – Chicago
54 East Walton Street
Chicago, IL 60611
(312) 649-0080

Bryan Wark
2nd Street Holdings, Inc.
628 San Quan Avenue
Venice, CA 90291
(310) 396-9072

*The entrance to the opulent world of Bountiful,
the home of Sue Balmforth.*

PERIODICALS:

Antique Journal
1684 Decoto Road, Suite 166
Union City, CA 95487
(800) 791-8592; (510) 791-8592

Northern California, Oregon, and Nevada
Monthly newspaper, available free at 1,500
California locations, stores, auctions, and bookstores.

Antiques and Collectibles
500 Fesler Street, Suite 201
El Cajon, CA 92020
(619) 593-2925

Southern California, Arizona, and Nevada
Monthly newspaper, available free at antiques malls
and stores.

Antique Trader
P.O. Box 1050
Dubuque, IA 52004
(800) 334-7165

Weekly national publication, sold by subscription.
Classified, calendar of shows, markets, and
auctions listed by state.

Clark's Flea Market USA
5469 Inland Cove Court
Milton, FL 32583
(850) 623-0794

National directory of events, sold by
subscription, published four times a year.

Maine Antique Digest
P.O. Box 1429
911 Main Street
Waldoboro, ME 04572
(800) 752-8521

East Coast monthly periodical, sold by subscription.
Classified, calendar of shows by advertisers.
U.S. and international listings.

Cotton & Quail Antique Trail
P.O. Box 326
Monticello, FL 32345
(800) 757-7755; (850) 997-3880

Covers the nine Southern states: Kentucky, Tennessee,
North Carolina, South Carolina, Alabama, Georgia,
Florida, Mississippi, and Louisiana. Monthly antique
periodical with four-month auction and show calendar.

Warman's Today's Collector
700 East State Street
Iola, WI 54990-0001
(800) 258-0929

National monthly publication, for sale at newsstands.
Articles, events listed by state, and classified section.

BOOKS

Antique Atlas
By Ken Leggett
Rainy Day Publishing Co.
Sourcebook with state-by-state listing of
antiques shops across the United States.

Price Guide to
Flea Market Treasures
By Harry L. Rinker Jr.
Krause Publishing
List of choice U.S. flea markets and publications.

Maloney's Antiques and
Collection Resource Directory
By David Maloney
Antique Trader Books

The Official Directory to U.S. Flea Markets
Edited by Kitty Werner
House of Collectibles

U.S. Flea Market Directory
By Albert La Farge
Avon Books

FLEA-MARKET LISTINGS

CALIFORNIA
LONG BEACH:
Long Beach Outdoor Antique & Collectible Market

Long Beach Veterans Stadium at Lakewood Boulevard & Conant Street   (213) 655-5703

Hours: Third Sunday of every month, 6:30 a.m. to 3:00 p.m. Extra show first Sunday in November.
Admission: $4.50 per person. Early bird rate: 5:30 a.m.to 6:30 a.m., $10.00. Free parking.
"Antiques and collectibles, averaging over 800 vendors."

PASADENA:
Rose Bowl Flea Market

1001 Rose Bowl Drive at Rosemont Avenue & Arroyo Boulevard   (213) 560-7469

Hours: Second Sunday of every month, 9:00 a.m. to 3:00 p.m.
Admission: $5.00 per person after 9:00 a.m. Free parking.
$10.00 entry at 7:30 a.m. $15.00 entry at 6:00 a.m.

California's largest flea market, with reportedly 2,200 vendors. The general public enters after 9:00 a.m., but for a higher entry fee you can get in for the preview hour, starting at 6:00 a.m.

SAN BERNADINO:
San Bernardino Swap Meet / Outdoor Market

At the National Orange Showgrounds / 689 South East Street   (909) 888-6788

Hours: Every Sunday, 6:00 a.m. to 3:00 p.m.
Admission: $1.00 per person. Children under 12 free.
Free parking available. In addition, the fourth Sunday of every month is the heritage Antique Memory Lane show on the same site, included in price of admission.

More than thirty-seven years in operation, this outdoor market has upwards of 1,000 vendors, many nondealers just weeding out their own stock.

SANTA MONICA:
Santa Monica Outdoor Antique & Collection Market

Airport Avenue, south side of the Santa Monica Airport, off Bundy   (213) 933-2511

Hours: Fourth Sunday of every month, 6:00 a.m. to 3:00 p.m.
Admission: 6:00 a.m. to 8:00 a.m., $5.00. 8:00 a.m. to 3:00 p.m., $3.50. Free parking

About 200 vendors with upscale merchandise.

VENTURA:
Ventura Flea Market and Swap Meet

At the Ventura County Fairgrounds   (213) 560-7469

Hours: Seven times a year, call for dates. 9:00 a.m. to 3:00 p.m.
Admission: $4.00 per person. Free parking.

Over 800 vendors, rain or shine.

CONNECTICUT
FARMINGTON:
Farmington Antiques Weekend

At the Farmington Polo Grounds, ten miles west of Hartford, three miles from I-84, exit 39.
(860) 677-7862

Hours: Second weekend of June and Labor Day weekend, 7:00 a.m. to 5:00 p.m.
Admission: $5.00 per person after 10:00 a.m. $20.00 early entry. Free parking.

Farmington is a national event, held outdoors and in tents, which specializes in early American rural antiques, furniture, and household goods.

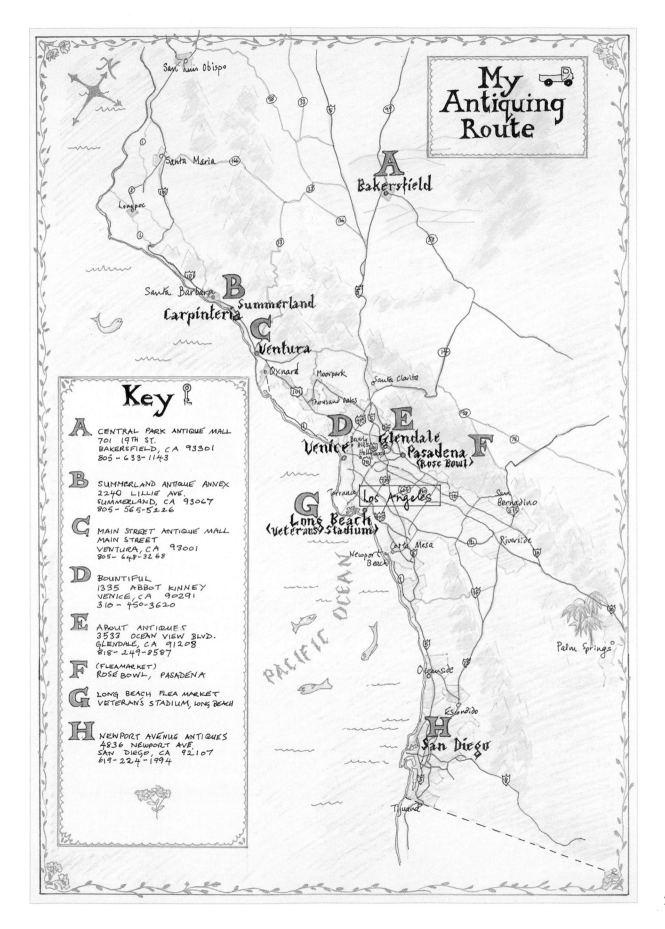

My Antiquing Route

San Luis Obispo

Santa Maria
Lompoc

A Bakersfield

Santa Barbara
B Summerland
Carpinteria
C Ventura
Oxnard   Moorpark   Santa Clarita
Thousand Oaks

D Venice   E Glendale
Beverly Hills   Pasadena
Hollywood   (Rose Bowl) F
San Bernadino

Torrance   Los Angeles
G Long Beach   Costa Mesa   Riverside
(Veteran's Stadium)
Newport Beach

PACIFIC OCEAN

Palm Springs

Oceanside

Escondido

H San Diego

Tijuana

Key

A CENTRAL PARK ANTIQUE MALL
701 19TH ST.
BAKERSFIELD, CA 93301
805-633-1143

B SUMMERLAND ANTIQUE ANNEX
2240 LILLIE AVE.
SUMMERLAND, CA 93067
805-565-5226

C MAIN STREET ANTIQUE MALL
MAIN STREET
VENTURA, CA 93001
805-648-3268

D BOUNTIFUL
1335 ABBOT KINNEY
VENICE, CA 90291
310-450-3620

E ABOUT ANTIQUES
3533 OCEAN VIEW BLVD.
GLENDALE, CA 91208
818-249-8587

F (FLEAMARKET)
ROSE BOWL, PASADENA

G LONG BEACH FLEA MARKET
VETERAN'S STADIUM, LONG BEACH

H NEWPORT AVENUE ANTIQUES
4836 NEWPORT AVE.
SAN DIEGO, CA 92107
619-224-1994

MASSACHUSETTS

BRIMFIELD:

Crystal Brook Antique Show (413) 245-7647
J & J Promotions Antiques & Collectibles Shows (413) 245-3436
New England Motel Antiques Market (508) 347-2179
Shelton Antique Shows (413) 245-3591

Route 20, near Sturbridge

Hours: Held three times a year (usually beginning the second Tuesday of May, the Tuesday after the Fourth of July, and the Tuesday after Labor Day in September). Market runs from dawn on Tuesday through 5:00 p.m. Sunday. Call for exact dates.
Admission: Varies from free to $5.00. Parking is usually around $5.00.

The Brimfield market is actually a series of about 22 markets that run more or less consecutively over five days in May, July, and September. It is virtually a whole town full of antiques and collectibles with some 400 vendors spread over many acres of land. It is often referred to as the best market in the country.

MICHIGAN

ANN ARBOR:

Ann Arbor Antiques Market

5055 Ann Arbor Saline Road. Exit 175 off I-94, go south three miles
Ann Arbor, MI 48103
(313) 662-9453

Hours: Third Sunday of the month, April–November. 6:00 a.m. to 4:00 p.m.
Extra shows in April and November. Admission: $5.00 per person. Free parking.

30 years in operation, 350 dealers of good-quality antiques. All dealers screened and referenced.

NEW MEXICO

SANTA FE:

Trader Jack's Flea Market

Seven miles north of Santa Fe on Highway 285   (505) 455-7874

Hours: Every Friday, Saturday, and Sunday, 7:00 a.m. to 6:00 p.m. Free parking.

This flea market operates about nine months a year, weather permitting. Open since 1975.

SOUTH CAROLINA

CHARLESTON:

Low County Flea Market & Collectibles

77 Calhoun Street at the Gaillard Auditorium
(803) 884-7204 / 577-7400

Hours: Third weekend of every month and one extra in late November.
Saturdays, 9:00 a.m. to 6:00 p.m. Sundays, 10:00 a.m. to 5:00 p.m. Admission: $2.00 per person

Mostly antiques, collectibles, and estate merchandise.

TENNESSE
NASHVILLE:
Tennessee State Fairgrounds Flea Market

At the Tennessee State Fairgrounds, at Wedgewood   (615) 862-5016

Hours: Fourth weekend of every month, except in December, when it is held
on the third weekend. Saturdays, 6:00 a.m. to 6: 00 p.m. Sundays, 7:00 a.m. to 4:00 p.m.
Admission: $2.00 per person

Mostly antiques, collectibles, and estate merchandise.

INTERNATIONAL

For the international listings it is always a good idea to check the dates and times. Mornings are generally
a better bet, because things can wind down early. Many cities have weekly or monthly markets. Ask at
your hotel for information about local events.

LONDON:
Bermondsey Market (or New Caledonia Market)

South of Tower Bridge / Bermondsey Street and Long Lane. • Hours: 4:00 a.m. to afternoon.

Brick Lane Market

Shoreditch tube station, in East End. • Hours: Sundays, 9:00 a.m.to 2:00 p.m.

Camden Lock Market

Camden Town tube station, Northern Line. • Hours: Sundays, 9:00 a.m. to 5:00 p.m.

Camden Passage Market (Camden Walk Market)

Angel tube station, turn right, then right again. • Hours: Saturdays and Wednesdays, 8:00 a.m. to 4:00 p.m.

Petticoat Lane

Middlesex Street in East End, Liverpool Street, Aldgate, or Aldgate East stop.
Hours: Sundays, early to noon (best time).

Portobello Road

West end of London, Notting Hill Gate tube stop.
Hours: Saturdays, 5:30 a.m. to 3:00 p.m. for the outdoor market; shops open daily.

PARIS:
Porte de Cligancourt/Marche aux Puces

Metro Station: Porte de Cligancourt
Hours: Saturday–Monday, 9:30 a.m. to 6:00 p.m.

The largest flea market in Europe, with more than 1,600 sellers. This location also has a number of
satellite markets along its edges comprising several miles of great shopping.

SOME OF MY FAVORITE RESOURCES

CALIFORNIA

About Antiques
3533 Ocean View Boulevard
Glendale, CA 91208
(818) 249-8587

Good mix of old things, no reproductions. American furniture, special vintage textile section with trims and buttons, decorative accessories, pottery, and antique holiday items.

Annie, Fannie, and Abigail
Vintage Collections
320 Manhattan Beach Boulevard
Manhattan Beach, CA 90266
(310) 379-7911

Eclectic selection of vintage furniture, architectural pieces, garden, lighting, and lamps from the 1900s to today.

Antique Alley
706 State Street
Santa Barbara, CA 93101
(805) 962-3944

Music of yesteryear entertains in this antiques mall whose dealers show a mix of jewelry, furniture, and decorative items from the turn of the century to the 1970s.

Antique Chase
2350 Lillie Avenue
Summerland, CA 93067
(805) 565-2176

Painted furniture, wicker, pottery, quilts, English tins, and ironstone.

Attic Treasures
337 East Main Street
Ventura, CA 93001
(805) 641-1039

Collective with about fifteen dealers specializing in higher-end antiques, silver, furniture, pottery, lamps, mirrors, and jewelry. All merchandise more than 100 years old.

Beau Rivage Antiques
2264 Lillie Avenue
Summerland, CA 93067
(805) 969-5444

Store with cottage-style furniture, antiques, and garden furniture and accessories.

Beverly's Closet /Beverly Schmidt
5452 Adobe Falls Road #8
San Diego, CA 92120-4422
(619) 582-6888

Vintage linens of all kinds and women's clothing and accessories shown at the Vintage Fashion Expo–Santa Monica, and the Textile, Costume, and Clothing show–Burbank

Bountiful
1335 Abbot Kinney Boulevard
Venice, CA 90291
(310) 450-3620

Sells architectural elements and American painted furniture, 19th-century French pieces, and opulent Italian lighting.

Central Park Antique Mall
701 19th Street
Bakersfield, CA 93301
(805) 633-1143

Eighty-nine different dealers, showing higher-end antiques and collectibles, furniture, accessories, and vintage toys. No crafts.

Crawfords Warehouse
4401 Soquel Drive
Soquel, CA 95073
(408) 462-1528

Family owned and operated for more than 25 years,
selling antique painted furniture found in their home state
of Pennsylvania. All original old milk-paint-finish furniture
and architectural pieces.

Great American Antiques
625 19th Street
Bakersfield, CA 93301
(805) 322-1776

38,500-square-foot antiques mall with eleven dealers.
Lots of furniture, bookcases, and unusual items,
including entire pubs and bars made of old wood.

Heirlooms Antique Mall
327 East Main Street
Ventura, CA 93001
(805) 648-4833

Thirty dealers in 5,000-square-foot with furniture and household
accessories and a sprinkling of antiques.

Little Treasures, at Antiques & More
327 Pine Avenue
Long Beach, CA 90802
(562) 437-3040

Shop within another store, specializing in vintage
clothing and accessories. They also sell at various
shows and markets in the area.

Liz's Antique Hardware
453 South La Brea
Los Angeles, CA 90036
(213) 939-4403

Original antique hardware from the 1850s to the 1950s
for doors, windows, curtains, and furniture. Antique
lighting and bath accessories. Contemporary and
reproduction hardware also available.

Moss Landing Antique & Trading Co.
P.O. Box 478
Moss Landing Road
Moss Landing, CA 95039
(408) 633-3988

Six dealers, each in their own room, with unique and one-
of-a-kind items. Many of their customers are other dealers.

Newport Avenue Antique
4836 Newport Avenue
San Diego, CA 92107
(619) 224-1994

Large selection, with 40 dealers. Includes signed
costume jewelry, western goods, furniture,
lighting fixtures, and sconces.

Newport Avenue Antique Center
4864 Newport Avenue
San Diego, CA 92107
(619) 222-8686

18,000-square-foot, with 170 dealers. They have everything.
Antiques and collectibles in the Ocean Beach Antique District.

Nicholby Antique Mall
404 East Main Street
Ventura, CA 93001
(805) 653-1195

About 40 dealers showing furniture and accessories.
Good variety, good prices.

Ocean Beach Antique Mall
4878 Newport Avenue
San Diego, CA 92107
(619) 223-6170

Two stories tall with up to 40 dealers, this mall features traditional American and distressed furniture, accessories, pottery, old hardware, and dollhouses.

Somewhere In Time Antiques
1312 19th Street
Bakersfield, CA 93301
(805) 326-8562

Store with a little bit of everything: pottery, glassware, pitchers, clothing, furniture, etc.

State Street Antique Mall
710 State Street
Santa Barbara, CA 93101
(805) 967-2575

More than 50 dealers with a wide a variety of goods: furniture, vintage linens and clothes, fabrics, antique phones, paintings, and household accessories.

Summerland Hillside Antiques
P.O. Box 1434
Summerland, CA 93067
(805) 565-5226
(805) 565-5226

Antiques, interiors, and treasures. This store features mirrors, lamps, and furniture, from cottage-style to formal.

Tiffany's Antiques
3010 North Center Street
Soquel, CA 95073
(408) 477-9808

Collective with 13 dealers showing a varied selection of cottage- and garden-style, vintage florals, ironwork, pine, oak, and wicker, painted pieces, and lampshades.

Tutti-Fruitti
Diana Weihs
(213) 733-3123

Vintage clothing from the 1930s to 1950s, sold at antiques shows throughout the Los Angeles area.

Vignettes
4828 Newport Avenue
San Diego, CA 92107
(619) 222-9244

Displays set up like rooms and gardens, selling vintage linens and clothing, jewelry, unusual architectural items, ironworks, and furniture from the 1850s to the 1950s.

ARIZONA

The Brass Armadillo
12419 North 28th Drive
I-17 north of Cactus
Phoenix, AZ 85029
(888) 942-0030

610 dealers in 40,000 square-feet. Furniture, architectural items, lighting, and 612 glass-enclosed cases with hundreds of treasures.

CONNECTICUT

Wright's Barn
Wright Road off Route 4
Torrington, CT 06790
(203) 482-0095

An indoor market in a 10,000-square-foot barn with 40 permanent dealers.

IOWA

The Brass Armadillo
701 N.E. 50th Avenue
Des Moines, IA 50313
(515) 262-0092

Large antiques mall housing 400 dealers in 36,000 square feet. Glass, pottery, furniture, and much more.

MICHIGAN

Great Midwestern Antique Emporium
5233 Dixie Highway
Waterford, MI 48329
(248) 623-7460

5,000-square-foot co-op mall housing 50 dealers. Antiques and collectibles—depression glass, pottery, and furniture, from the 1850s to the 1950s.

Kalik's Antiques
198 West Liberty
Plymouth, MI 48329
(313) 455-5595

Eight dealers in the Old Village part of Plymouth featuring military, western, sports, hunting, and fishing antiques; furniture; and collectibles.

NEBRASKA

The Brass Armadillo
10666 Sapp Brothers Drive
Omaha, NE 68138
(800) 896-9140

Another large mall from Brass Armadillo. 350 dealers in 30,000 square feet of space, which features their furniture and selection of books.

NEW MEXICO

El Colectivo
De Vargas Mall / corner of
Passe de Peralta and North Guadeloupe
Santa Fe, NM 87501
(505) 820-7205

Antiques mall with 16 permanent dealers and additional merchandise on consignment. Antiques, collectibles, and out-of-print books.

Majestic Lion Antique Center
5048 2nd Avenue
Des Moines, IA 50313
(515) 282-5466

High-end antiques in a 250-dealer mall. They offer American furniture, accessories, porcelain, pottery, glass, and the entire 35,000-square-foot ceiling full of lighting fixtures.

NEW YORK

Olde Good Things
124 West 24th Street
New York, NY 10011-1904
(212) 989-8401

Solomon's Mine
95 Main Street
Cold Springs, NY 10516
(914) 265-5042

ENGLAND

The Old Haberdasher
141 Portobello Road
Nottinghill Gate
London W11
0181-907-8684

Architectural artifacts salvaged from old New York buildings.
Huge inventory of doorknobs, doors, mantels, hardware,
sinks, tubs, gates, stonework, fences, columns, and a lot more.

Unusual antiques and collectibles. Old medical equipment
and furniture, cameras, mechanical and optical items.

Antique lace, braids, ribbons, trims, and haberdashery.

*The evidence of this hard work makes me think twice
about whether it's fair to bargain too hard.*

*Mission accomplished. Cathy, Pete, and I have just completed
an early morning flea-market buying trip.*

The Divine Ladder

Unto each mortal who comes to earth
A ladder is given by God at birth
And up this ladder every soul must go,
Step by step from the Valley below;
Step by step to the Center of space,
On this ladder of lives, to the Starting place.

In time departed (which yet endures)
I shape my ladder, and you shape yours,
Whatever they are --- they are what we made
A ladder of light, or a ladder of shade,
A ladder of love, or a hateful thing,
A ladder of strength, or a wavering string,
A ladder of gold, or a ladder of straw,
Each is a ladder of a righteous Law.
We flung them away at the Call of Death,
We took them again with the next life breath,
For a Keeper stands at the great birth gates;
As each soul passes, its ladder waits.

Tho mine be narrow, and yours be broad,
On my ladder alone can I climb to God.
On your ladder alone can your feet ascend,
For none may borrow and none may lend.
If toil and trouble and pain are found,
Twisted and corded to form each round,
If rusting iron or mouldering wood
Is the fragile frame, you must make it good;
You must build it over and fashion it strong,
Tho the task be as hard as your life is long;
For up this ladder the pathway leads
To earthly pleasures and spirit needs;
And all that may come in another way
Shall be but illusion and will not stay

In useless effort, then waste no time;
Rebuild your ladder, and Climb and Climb

The end.

NOTES